GOD'S SPIRIT
at
WORK

LESSONS FROM THE MISSION FIELD

BARRY D. VOSS

Xulon Press
2301 Lucien Way #415
Maitland, FL 32751
407.339.4217
www.xulonpress.com

God's Spirit at Work
Lessons From the Mission Field

Unless otherwise indicated, Scripture quotations taken
from the Holy Bible, New International Version (NIV).
Copyright © 1973, 1978, 1984, 2011 by Biblica, Inc.™.
Used by permission. All rights reserved.

Printed in the United States of America

Paperback ISBN-13: 978-1-6322-1107-1
Ebook ISBN-13: 978-1-6322-1108-8

TABLE OF CONTENTS

PROLOGUE

"So I say, live by the Spirit, and you will not gratify the desires of the sinful nature."
Galatians 5:16

Several years ago, I wrote a book about how my life was transformed by God. It tells the story of how I went from being a believer in Christ to becoming a follower of Christ. It was entitled ***Transformed: Learning to Live by Faith*** (Xulon Press, 2013). In that book I detailed how my encounter with the God of the Universe changed my life and how faith in His Son, Jesus Christ, was the catalyst for that transformation. I described my own personal journey of faith and how God was preparing me and guiding me to full time ministry through various elements in my life story, such as my church involvement, my education, my career, my family and my travels.

The underlying subject of that book was my faith, and how putting my trust in Jesus allowed God to use my life for His purposes and not mine. It also gave me an opportunity to see God's hand on my life through various trials and struggles. Without faith in Christ, my life would be very different today. I would probably be retiring from a lengthy business career with not much more than a pension, an IRA, and a few insignificant work accomplishments to show for it.

Instead, because I chose to follow Jesus, my life has been filled with more blessings than I can count! And I have the knowledge that God has been using me to impact the world for His glory through our ministry of training and equipping pastors and church leaders (*see our FaithLife Ministries website at* **www.faithlifeministries.net**).

While that book described the process by which God transformed my life and led me from a business career to ministry work, in this book I want to share how God has impacted my life in that ministry through His Holy Spirit.

The last chapter of my previous book was entitled, "Catching the Wave." I used body surfing and catching a wave as a metaphor for following Christ. I wanted to *"catch the wave"* of the Holy Spirit in my life to carry me forward to experiencing an abundant life with Jesus. Now that my life has been transformed from being a believer of Jesus into a follower of Jesus, the next phase would be to submit to His Spirit and let Him have control of my life.

I have known for a long time that it is much easier to confess our faith in Jesus than to put our complete trust in Him and do what He asks of us. There is often a big difference between what we say we believe and then how we actually live. As Jesus said to his disciples in the garden of Gethsemane, *"The spirit is willing, but the body is weak."* (**Matthew 26:41**)

The reality is that we were never meant to follow Him on our own power. God not only gives us His Holy Spirit to enable us to have faith in Him, but He also gives us that same Holy Spirit to enable us to obey

Him and do what He asks. As the Bible says, *"Not by might, not by power, but by my Spirit says the Lord."* (**Zechariah 4:6**) So, the only way we can truly be followers of Jesus is to allow God's Holy Spirit access to our hearts and minds, and to let Him guide us according to His will. We cannot follow Jesus by our own will or power, but only through God's Holy Spirit!

For a large part of my life, I have not really thought much about the Holy Spirit. Most of my spiritual focus was on God and my salvation through His Son, Jesus. Nevertheless, as I was growing up, I was taught about the triune God (the Father, Son and Holy Spirit). As a matter of fact, the church I attended as a child was named Holy Trinity Lutheran Church. So, the Trinity is something that I have known about all of my life and have professed whenever I say the Apostle's Creed. However, I have not embraced the role of the Holy Spirit in my life and faith as much as God and Jesus. It seemed that the only time I thought about the Holy Spirit was on Pentecost, when our church would celebrate the coming of the Holy Spirit to the disciples.

But after my personal encounter with the Holy Spirit in the mission field at age 42, I began to realize the importance of the Holy Spirit in my life and His significance to my spiritual growth. Jesus told His disciples, *"But the Counselor, the Holy Spirit, whom the Father will send in my name, will teach you all things and will remind you of everything I have said to you."* (**John 14:26**) Jesus was assuring us that although He would be ascending to Heaven, He would not be leaving us alone or without God's power. God would send His Holy Spirit, the third person of His Trinity, to help us, walk with us, strengthen us and guide us in our lives.

Since that encounter, I have tried to submit my life to the Holy Spirit so that I could have God's power in my life and ministry. While I admit that I don't always submit every area of my life to God, I am now more acutely aware of the Holy Spirit and intentionally call upon Him for help and guidance much more frequently. And now I can't imagine not taking advantage of what the Holy Spirit can do when I call upon Him.

I have been training and serving pastors and church leaders on the international mission field in the majority world for 24 years now. In that time I have been on 137 short term mission trips to 50 different nations. On these trips, I have experienced God's presence and Holy Spirit on many occasions and in many different ways. I have seen the Holy Spirit at work. I have watched God use other people in ways that they themselves thought were not possible. I have seen God bring about His purpose in ways that I could not have ever imagined. As I reflect upon the work of God and His Spirit in my life and ministry, I realize that I have learned many lessons from Him that are worth sharing.

I believe it is important for everyone to understand how God, through His Holy Spirit, intersects with our lives on a daily basis when we call upon Him. God is not absent nor is His Spirit distant from us. Jesus said, *"Ask and it will be given to you; seek and you will find; knock and the door will be opened to you. For everyone who asks, receives; he who seeks, finds; and to him who knocks, the door will be opened."* (**Matthew 7:7-8**) God is ever present in our time of need, and His Spirit is ready and willing to give us His wisdom, protection and provision when we call upon Him.

Living by faith in Jesus teaches us how to trust God. Living by the Holy Spirit teaches us how to submit our lives to Him and to experience life to its fullest. Jesus lived by the Holy Spirit and said, *"The thief comes only to steal and kill and destroy; I have come that they may have life, and have it to the full."* (**John 10:10**)

It is my prayer that you will find these stories and spiritual experiences of mine inspiring. It is also my hope that they will encourage you to submit your life to His Holy Spirit as well, and *"catch the wave"* right along with me!

Chapter 1

WHERE IS THE MISSION FIELD?

*"But you will receive power when the Holy Spirit
comes on you; and you will be my witnesses in
Jerusalem, and in all Judea and Samaria,
and to the ends of the earth."*
Acts 1:8

The mission field for the Christian is often misunderstood and sometimes misrepresented. Many
people have a limited view of the mission field and only
see it as less developed cultures, remote people groups,
Islamic nations, or nations in the 10/40 Window (the
part of the world between 10° and 40° latitude north
of the equator). While these are places where the mission field exists, they are not all of them. In actuality,
the mission field is all around us. The mission field is
wherever people live that do not know Jesus Christ or
believe in Him.

The western nations of the world have for many
years sent missionaries to Africa, Asia and Latin
America. These were generally areas of the world
that were considered less civilized and needed to be

1

developed and "Christianized" if they were to succeed and prosper. Many of the early missionaries from England and Europe, such as Stanley Livingston, actually went to help nations develop both economically and spiritually. They believed that Christianity and economic prosperity went together, and by spreading God's Word along with the gospel they could help nations develop economically as well. That was not a bad strategy. It resulted in many people becoming Christians and many nations developing economically at the same time.

As a matter of fact, today, there are more Christians in the southern hemisphere than in Europe and North America (*The Christian Century, Sara Miller, July 17, 2002*). Christianity was one of the major factors behind the democracies of western nations and their rise to global economic dominance in the 19th and 20th centuries. Their missionary efforts worked so well that they changed the dynamics of church growth from one area of the world to another!

Today, church attendance and Christian populations are declining in the northern hemisphere while they are growing in the southern hemisphere. While the growth in the southern hemisphere is cause for celebration, it is also a wake-up call for North America and Europe to not allow Christianity, and the spiritual influence of the Church, to dwindle away in the northern hemisphere. There must be a renewed focus on rebuilding the Church there as well.

In other words, the mission field is not just in Africa, Asia and Latin America anymore. While most people associate the mission field with foreign missions, the mission field is, in reality, all around us. It is no longer confined to certain regions of the world or nations of the world. There are people everywhere who need to know Jesus and have the opportunity to hear the gospel. But if our attention is only focused on other nations, we will miss the opportunity to share the good news with our neighbors, coworkers and fellow citizens.

A recent national study showed that about one half of all Americans no longer attend a church or consider themselves to have any religious faith (*Barna Research, Five Trends Defining Americans' Relationship to Churches, February 19, 2020*). This is a dramatic change from just two decades ago. That same study also showed that Americans have a low perception of the Church as an institution. And yet they are still seeking a spiritual connection. Unfortunately, it is not always from the Christian Church. Today, it is estimated that the USA is the 3rd largest mission field in the world (*Christian Today, Lillian Kwon, December 30, 2006*)!

Jesus told His disciples where the mission field was. He said to them, ***"But you will receive power when the Holy Spirit comes on you; and you will be my witnesses in Jerusalem, and in all Judea and Samaria, and to the ends of the earth."*** (**Acts 1:8**) What He was telling them clearly indicates that the mission field for His followers (Christians) is comprised of three locations – "Jerusalem, Judea & Samaria, and the ends of the earth." What exactly does that mean for Christians today?

First, it means that the mission field is **local** (*"Jerusalem"*). There are people in our local communities who don't know Jesus. Some of them are immigrants from other nations and cultures and may have never heard the gospel. Some may have grown up in an unchurched home. Some are young enough to have spurned Christianity by its social reputation or have never been exposed to it personally. Whatever the reason, the mission field is local.

Second, the mission field is also **regional & national** (*"Judea & Samaria"*). There are people who live in other states in our nation who likewise came from other countries and may never have heard of Jesus. They too may have had no church background or experience. Despite our global reputation for being a Christian nation, in some parts of America Christianity is no longer a major part of the culture. Some places are even quite hostile to the Christian faith. The percentage of Christians by state also varies all across our nation. Consequently, every part of America is a mission field!

Third, the mission field is **international** (*"the ends of the earth"*). There are many nations in the world that have other religions as their cultural foundation. Two examples might be India (Hindi) and Japan (Shintoism). They are an obvious mission field for Christianity. Some nations are even quite dangerous for Christians due to the fervent resistance to any religion that does not conform to their cultural heritage. A couple of examples might be Iran (Islam) and Myanmar (Buddhism). There are also former Communist nations that once denied all religion and have since become more fertile ground for the gospel. These are nations such as Russia and other former soviet republics like the Ukraine, Romania and Latvia. And let us not forget existing communist nations like North Korea that make Christianity against the law.

When people talk about missions, they are often referring to only this third part of the mission field– the international one. When people say they went on a mission trip we would normally assume that they went to another country. While that may often be the case, it is not representative of the true mission field. Many

Christians may not think they are on the mission field when they serve others during a crisis, such as victims of Hurricane Katrina in New Orleans. Yet, that too is a mission trip.

I was also guilty of that kind of thinking. I used to tell people that I went on my very first mission trip in 1996 to the nation of Kazakhstan. But that was not my first trip to the mission field, only my first *international* mission trip. I still recall visiting an orphanage in Illinois as a teenager with my church youth group to share the gospel and God's love. We also shared the gospel through Christmas caroling in our local community. I also remember participating with our church choir in a televised broadcast in Chicago where we shared the gospel through music and the Word. In other words, I was in the mission field doing local missions long before I realized it!

I've also been involved in the regional & national mission field. I went to Kentucky with my daughter and our church youth group to minister to poor Appalachian families and to help repair their mobile homes. I currently serve as a teacher with a homeless ministry in the inner city of Atlanta. I lead them in monthly Bible studies and occasional worship time with my guitar. I also use my personal Facebook page to share God's Word through weekly postings that go to all my friends all over America. The internet is a great vehicle that we can all use to share the gospel, and our faith, throughout our state and nation.

Although most of my mission field activities have been in the international arena through our ministry of training pastors and church leaders globally, that in no way relinquishes my obligation to reach the local, regional and national mission field as well. I think if we all begin to see the mission field as something that is all around us, we can then take advantage of the opportunities that God provides us right where we are. This is because He has deployed us where we live and work to share the gospel, serve others, and grow God's kingdom without ever having to travel far.

It is much easier, less costly and more convenient to serve those who are right around us than to travel abroad. There are typically no language barriers, foreign currencies, or cultural differences to learn or adapt to. There are no lengthy flights or multiple time zone adjustments to overcome. And if we become uncomfortable for any reason, we can quickly get home.

But the international mission field should not be ignored either. Short-term international mission trips afford three distinct advantages that a local or national mission trip cannot offer or duplicate.

First, short term international mission trips push us out of our comfort zone and force us to put more trust in God. When we are halfway around the world we just can't turn around and go home. It is going to make us uncomfortable. But that's the point. When we don't know the language, don't like the food, or can't just leave, our only option is to turn to God and rely on Him to help us through it. That's something we don't always experience in the mission field in our own country. As a result, when we go to a foreign nation, we are more likely to reach out to God for His provision and protection.

Second, short term international mission trips enable us to gain a different perspective on the rest of the world. In America, we live in a culture of affluence, confidence and self-centeredness. When we visit other nations, we can see first-hand how other people live, how they struggle, and how they rely on God just to survive. That causes us to reflect upon our blessings as Americans, and to realize how much we have in comparison to the rest of the world. As a result, we start to look at other people the way that God looks at them. And that often leads us to re-evaluate our priorities in life and to focus on what God wants us to do rather than what we want to do.

Third, short term international mission trips allow us to take the time to focus on God for a week or two. When we are at home, the cares of the world, our personal burdens, and our long to-do list often take top priority. That tends to squeeze God out of our lives. But when we go on a trip to serve others in another nation, our focus tends to be on them, and God. That allows us to grow in our faith, experience God's hand in our service, and see how the Holy Spirit works in us and through others. For me, this has had the biggest impact on my life, and is the subject of much of the content of this book.

So, where is the mission field? It is everywhere and all around us. That's it. It's simple, it's readily available, and it's waiting for us. We don't even have to look hard for it. We only need to open our eyes and hearts to the opportunities that God presents to us to share our faith in Jesus or serve others in need.

At this point, you may be thinking about your own mission field. Where is it? Where is God calling you to serve others? It might be in your community, where you work, or where you go to school. It could be a nationwide ministry serving the poor, feeding the hungry, or providing relief to those impacted by a disaster. Maybe God is presenting opportunities for you to go to the foreign mission field and calling you to leave your comfort zone for Him and His purpose.

God has a mission field for every follower of Christ. But it is up to each of us to seek God in prayer to discover where He would call us to go and serve others. I would encourage everyone who considers themselves a follower of Jesus to first recognize this calling, and then to pray for God's direction for your life. God will reveal your mission field to you if you will only ask Him.

Chapter 2

WE ARE NEVER ALONE

"Where can I go from Your Spirit?
Where can I flee from Your presence?"
Psalm 139:7

One of the great truths of the Bible is that God is always with us. He never abandons us or leaves us to fend for ourselves. He proclaimed this promise to Joshua when He said to him, *"As I was with Moses, so I will be with you; I will never leave you nor forsake you."* (**Joshua 1:5**) His promise to Joshua is just as true for us today if we believe in His Son, Jesus. God created us to worship Him and to give Him glory. He loves us unconditionally and therefore would never cut us off from His presence. His greatest desire is to be with us, to walk with us, and to help us through our struggles in this world. And He does that through His Holy Spirit.

The Bible tells us that God is Spirit. It says, *"Now the earth was formless and empty, darkness was over the surface of the deep and the Spirit of God was hovering over the waters."* (**Genesis 1:2**) In other words, God is a Spirit that is present in the earth and the heavens. Furthermore, Jesus confirmed this when he

9

proclaims to the Samaritan woman at the well, *"God is spirit, and His worshipers must worship in spirit and in truth."* (**John 4:4**) He also told his disciples, *"But the Counselor, the Holy Spirit, whom the Father will send in my name, will teach you all things and remind you of everything I have said to you."* (**John 14:26**) Jesus is confirming that God and His Holy Spirit will be present wherever and whenever we need Him!

But there are many people who question where God is during their time of struggle. They don't seem to be able to feel His presence, or know that His Spirit is right there beside them. They pray but don't get a response. They think that God has other more important things to do than to help them in their time of trial. Perhaps they doubt that He *wants* to help them. But that is not who God is, nor is it what His Word says about Him.

There are several passages of Scripture that confirm God's presence with us. For example, the Bible says, *"Where can I go from Your Spirit? Where can I flee from Your presence? If I go up to the heavens, You are there; if I make my bed in the depths, You are there. If I rise on the wings of the dawn, if I settle on the far side of the sea, even there Your hand will guide me, Your right hand will hold me fast."* (**Psalm 139:7-8**) In other words, there is no place on this earth or in heaven where God's Spirit is not present with us.

We also read that *"You will seek me and find me when you seek me with all your heart."* (**Jeremiah 29:13**) This passage tells us that we must first seek Him if we desire His Spirit and His presence. He's right there, but His desire is that we seek Him first. Jesus confirmed this when he said, *"But seek first His kingdom and his righteousness, and all these things will be given to you as well."* (**Matthew 6:33**)

When we seek Him, God makes His presence known to us through His Spirit. His Word says, *"Come near to God and He will come near to you."* (**James 4:8**) God will not force Himself upon us. Instead, He waits patiently for us to come to Him. And when we come to Him, He responds to us as well. The Bible reminds us of that when it says, *"Let us then approach God's throne of grace with confidence, so that we may receive mercy and find grace to help us in our time of need."* (**Hebrews 4:16**) God's Word declares His spiritual presence when we call upon Him. He also promises to be with us and to help us in our time of need.

We generally experience God's Spirit in one of three ways. First, we experience His calming presence or His reassurance that He will see us through our present circumstances. Second, His Spirit can show up in our midst and make His presence known to us. Third, we hear His still small voice that speaks to us in our spirit and urges us to do something.

I experienced His Spirit in all three ways very dramatically on my first international mission trip, which was to the nation of Kazakhstan in April of 1996.

The first type of spiritual experience occurred upon my arrival into Kazakhstan. I had been out of the country before (mostly to Europe), but never to Central Asia. I had never even heard of Kazakhstan before I signed up to join the mission team. Although I had been to Russia in 1988 with an American tourist group, I really wasn't sure what to expect in this nation. All I knew was that it was part of the former Soviet Union. In Russia we stayed in modest hotels, ate good food, had clean buses, and official tour guides. I highly doubted that I would experience the same kind of luxuries on a low-budget Christian mission trip.

Our plane landed in the city of Almaty in the middle of the night, around 1 am. It was dark and felt ominous to me. The airport was small, dark and old, and there was only one small doorway leading into immigration. There were soldiers with machine guns standing guard inside and outside the terminal as well. After going through immigration (which also made me feel quite uncomfortable), I went to collect my luggage. The baggage claim area was not a big room and had only one carousel. I watched as many of my team members collected their bags and headed out of the terminal. I was one of the last ones to come out of the terminal because I had brought a guitar with me, which was the last item unloaded off the plane.

As I cleared the customs check, I walked out of that area with my suitcase, backpack and guitar through one small door. On the other side of the door was a room packed with people. It was so full I could not see any other members of our team of 29 Americans. Just then, an individual stepped forward who recognized the mission team tag on my suitcase. He just took my bag and motioned me to follow him outside. Not seeing anyone else from my team in the crowded arrival hall, I was apprehensive. But I decided to trust him and so I followed him.

As we left the terminal I began to wonder where he was leading me. I did not see any members of our team or a bus. I was a little scared and began to pray for God's protection and that I had made the right decision. I immediately felt God's Spirit and His calming presence. After walking for about two blocks, we rounded the corner of a building and I saw an old, run down bus with the rest of my team members. I was quite relieved and recall saying a quiet prayer of thanks to God for being with me. His spiritual presence had calmed me through a stressful time!

The second type of spiritual experience, however, would be much more eye-opening. Once on the bus we headed to our hotel across town. It had also started to rain. Our transportation was a 1960's era bus with old, uncomfortable seats and leaky air vents in the ceiling. Looking around I could tell that I was in a very different place. I felt like Dorothy in the *Wizard of Oz*–*"I'm not in Kansas anymore!"*

We arrived at our hotel around 3 am, but the door was locked. We then had to wait on the bus while our team leader went to find someone to let us in (our hotel was a recently converted sanitarium that did not have a 24-hour front desk). By the time someone came to let us in it was around 5 am.

While we waited in the lobby for our room keys, one of our team members suddenly falls to the floor and starts writhing and screaming. I thought to myself, *what on earth is going on here?* I then see our team leaders attend to her. They told the rest of us to get our keys and go to our rooms and that they would take care of her. It soon dawned on me that she was having a spiritual attack of some kind.

So, I went to my assigned room and waited for my roommate to show up. He was a pastor from St. Louis whom I had barely met on the flight over. When he didn't come up after I had unpacked and got settled in, I went back down to the lobby to inquire about him.

When I got to the lobby he was there with the woman, who now had calmed down. She was seated in a chair and was being attended to by my roommate. It turns out that he was her pastor and the one who invited her to come on the trip. I further learned that this woman had come from an occult background before becoming a Christian. Obviously, the spiritual conflict was raging inside of her when she arrived. I believe that God and Satan were battling over this woman's soul at that moment.

That's the first time I had ever witnessed any kind of spiritual or demonic attack, and it had my mind swirling. The Bible says, ***"For our struggle is not against flesh and blood, but against the powers of this dark world and against the spiritual forces of evil in the heavenly realms."*** (**Ephesians 6:12**) My world had been dramatically altered by what I had just witnessed. The presence of spiritual forces suddenly became very real to me. God was making His presence known as His Spirit fought for one of His children!

The leaders decided that she could not remain with the team as she would potentially be a distraction to our ministry there. So, they arranged to have her pastor take her back to the USA the next day. Consequently, I no longer had a roommate.

As I headed back to my room the experiences of this night made me feel alone and a little uneasy. *What was I getting myself into? What would the rest of this trip be like? How am I going to make it through the next two weeks? Will there be more of these types of spiritual experiences to come?* I prayed and thanked the Lord that night for His Spirit that calmed me when we arrived at the airport. I also thanked Him for letting me know there were spiritual forces out there I could not see, and that His Spirit would fight for me as well!

Growing up in America, I had never witnessed any kind of spiritual manifestation like I had that night. My arrival in Kazakhstan was my introduction to it. I would also have the third type of spiritual experience a little later on that trip when God audibly spoke to me.

The purpose of this mission trip was to conduct a training conference on church growth. It was led by Dr. Kent Hunter, the founder of Church Doctor Ministries. During our conference, some of the pastors who attended were invited to come forward and share their testimony. As I listened to the testimony of Achmed, a pastor from Uzbekistan who had been in jail and beaten for his faith in Christ, God's Spirit began to speak to me about my weak faith and lack of obedience to His Word. I realized that I was not living my faith like Achmed, but merely going through the motions.

You see, on the outside, I looked like a Christian. But on the inside, my heart was far from God. God was challenging me on my lack of faith in the same way Jesus challenged the faith of his disciples when a storm rose up on the Sea of Galilee. He said to them, *"You of little faith, why are you so afraid?"* (**Mathew 8:26**).

I, too, was afraid to live out my faith. God's Spirit then urged me to not only believe in His Son, but to follow Him as well. That experience is what caused me to renew my faith in Christ and to seek to serve Him and follow Him in all that I do. I am forever grateful to God for challenging me to get out of my comfort zone and to truly live for Him!

So, on my very first international mission trip I experienced the Holy Spirit comforting me, battling Satan, and speaking to me. It was quite a spiritual awakening to say the least!

There were also other types of spiritual experiences that I would encounter in the mission field that were evidence of God's presence.

One experience that I also witnessed on that first trip to Kazakhstan is what is known as being "slain in the spirit." For those who may not know what that means, it simply means becoming temporarily and completely overcome by the Holy Spirit when a pastor or another Christian prays over you or even touches you. The power of the Holy Spirit flowing through the person who is praying causes the individual to go into a state of semi-consciousness. One of our team members had the Holy Spirit flowing through her so powerfully that I saw person after person drop right after she just touched them! At first, I wondered what was happening. It took me a few minutes to realize that they were being slain in the spirit, something I had heard of before but had never seen in person.

On my second trip to Kazakhstan later that year I had that experience myself. A young worship leader named Sergei, who I had met on our first trip to Kazakhstan, wanted to pray for me. I knew him because he was the worship leader on my first trip there six months earlier. I was allowed to play guitar with him and the praise band on that trip and we developed a close relationship, even though we did not speak the same language.

As he prayed over me, I felt my legs going weak and that I was starting to lose consciousness. I tried very hard to fight it off, but after a few moments I finally let go and allowed myself to succumb to the Spirit. They slowly laid me on the floor. While I knew there were people around me, I literally could not move. I tried to get up but could not. The Holy Spirit had completely overcome my physical body. I was slain in the spirit.

After about five minutes of immobility I was finally able to get up on my feet. It was a wonderful experience and the only time that it has ever happened to me.

I'm not exactly sure what it is about, other than to be completely overcome by the Holy Spirit, but I no longer doubt that it is real!

I also had another encounter with the Holy Spirit speaking to me in the nation of Kyrgyzstan a few years later. I was part of a mission team that had gone to Bishkek to lead a worship conference. We learned that there was a woman there that had the gift of prophecy. She said she had a Word from the Lord and offered to speak to each member of our American mission team individually. When she came to me, she spoke a prophecy saying that I would become a teacher of many nations. At that time, I had not done much teaching and wasn't sure what that meant. But today I run a global training ministry that has trained over 50,000 pastors and leaders in 99 nations!

I believe that God spoke to me through her that day, and that His Spirit was calling me for the very first time to the ministry of training pastors and church leaders, even though I did not know it then! (You can view a video of this prophecy at http://faithlifeministries.net/ prophecy/).

My experience with spiritual manifestations was not limited to Central Asia. On one of my visits to Kenya I was attending the local Sunday morning worship service at the church of our host in the city of Nakuru. At one point during the service people were invited to come forward for individual prayer. One of them who went up for prayer was a woman who, while being prayed for, suddenly started screaming, fell to the floor and started writhing. This time I knew what this was!

Immediately the pastor and a couple of elders went to her and started praying over her feverishly in the name of Jesus. They were praying for her deliverance from a demonic spirit. I looked around the church and everyone else was still praying. They acted as if this was a regular occurrence at their church. It certainly wasn't for me!

As they prayed over this woman declaring the power and victory of Jesus she slowly began to relax and eventually was calm and lucid. I stood there amazed at what I had just witnessed for a second time. This was not an exorcism, but rather a group of believers praying for someone in the grip of a satanic spiritual force. At that instant, I realized that the *"spiritual forces of evil"* that the Apostle Paul wrote about to the Ephesians were just as real today as they were back then. I thought of the Scripture which says, ***"…resist the devil, and he will flee from you."*** (**James 4:7**) I was a witness to that truth!

The reason I share these experiences is because I have felt, witnessed and heard the Holy Spirit acting directly in my life. It is not an illusion. It is not something I sought. Rather, it is recognizing that the Holy Spirit is there to help us and make His presence known to us. Once I began to experience the presence of the Spirit in my life, it convinced me that I could no longer live without His Spirit! My life became one of trying to live more in His Spirit and to experience life more powerfully and abundantly. I believe this is exactly what the Apostle Paul meant when he said, ***"Since we live by the Spirit, let us keep in step with the Spirit."*** (**Galatians 5:25**)

If you are like me at all, you are probably aware of the Holy Spirit as the third person of the Trinity. Perhaps you often pray for the Spirit's peace and comfort amidst your trials and struggles in life. But have you experienced His presence in a way that causes you to desire more of Him in your daily life? Do you only seek the Holy Spirit when you are having difficulties, or do you reach out to Him in other facets of your life as well? Do you want to experience the power of the Holy Spirit in your life? It is my hope that you do.

I once heard a message from Dr. David Jeremiah on one of his radio broadcasts about the difference between physical and spiritual hunger. He said that with physical hunger, once we have eaten we fill up and no longer desire to continue eating. But with Spiritual hunger, once we eat of it we only desire to have more. I believe this is true. If you desire more of God and His Holy Spirit, then you will never have enough and will only want more. You will begin to experience the power of God's Spirit at work in your life and God will pour out His blessings on you in return. That's what happened to me, and it can happen to you!

Witnessing God's Spirit at work has taught me many things over the years, mostly through the many international mission trips that put me in the Lord's hands and allowed me to be more receptive to Him. Maybe it's just that I recognized His Spirit more often when I'm not at home and in my usual routine. Regardless of the reason, I have been very blessed by these spiritual experiences from the mission field that have shown me God's Spirit at work.

I have grouped these experiences into 10 spiritual lessons that I have learned as a result of witnessing God's Spirit at work. In the next ten chapters of this book, I will discuss each lesson and share experiences from my various mission trips that illustrate them. These lessons are as follows:

Lesson #1: God's Purpose Prevails
Lesson #2: God is Always at Work

Lesson #3: God Hears Our Prayers
Lesson #4: God Chooses Us
Lesson #5: God Provides for Us
Lesson #6: God Works through Us
Lesson #7: God Speaks for Us
Lesson #8: God Protects Us
Lesson #9: God Carries Us
Lesson #10: God is Always Faithful

It is my hope and prayer that you will find these lessons to be inspiring, encouraging and helpful as you seek to serve the Lord in your lives today. Furthermore, I pray that God will also reveal His Spirit to you so that you too will be able to acknowledge and experience His power, His reality, and His presence in your life!

Chapter 3

LESSON #1: GOD'S PURPOSE PREVAILS

"Many are the plans in a man's heart,
but it is the Lord's purpose that prevails."
Proverbs 19:21

S omeone once said, *"If you want to hear God laugh, tell him your plans."* That certainly seems true in my experience. I wrote an article recently for our ministry newsletter that I entitled, "Confessions of a Serial Planner." In the article I admitted that I plan everything. I like to plan and believe that it helps me to stay focused and accomplish what is important to me. I don't like to take trips, go to the store, or start a project without planning it out first. I want to have a plan to guide me and keep me on track so that I don't waste time or get distracted from my purpose.

Now to be clear, I don't always put together a detailed, multi-faceted project plan. Instead, I simply make a list of what I need to do. But if my goal is something more complex, like organizing a mission trip or developing a new ministry vision and plan, I put together a simple one page outline of what I need and when I must do it. That's all. By thinking through things ahead of time and having a plan, I believe I will be better prepared to handle obstacles and changes that come along that could impact my plan.

It is actually quite rare that a plan comes off the way it was intended. Even going to the grocery store often causes me to adjust my plan. For example, I always prepare a grocery list before I go to the store so that I make sure I get the things I need and don't forget anything. But many times, when I get to the store, I can't find what I am looking for, so I have to make a decision. Do I wait until I go shopping the next time or do I buy a similar product, which is often at a higher price? The decision could impact our monthly budget and what we set aside to pay for food for the month. Then there are the impulse purchases. As I walk down the aisle, I see something that looks good, or is on sale, and I add it to my shopping cart. Again, I must decide if I can afford the extra purchase or not.

The same is true for other plans, such as a mission trip, which are more complex. Most of the trips I organize today are fairly simple as they only involve two people, me and a training partner. My plan usually includes booking our airline tickets and hotels for the two of us. But I also have to communicate with a local host in the foreign country who organizes our local training conference, recruits attendees, arranges our local transportation, and prepares our materials for the training. Although I have a plan and a trip budget, they are often challenged by changes in flight schedules, airfares, hotel costs, training logistics, or other local issues, such as transportation.

So, even with a plan, there are always factors that can cause a change in the plan. Having a plan, however, allows me to make better decisions as these issues arise that must be dealt with. With a plan in place, I can determine what the impact of these conflicts would be on our goal or budget, and then make the necessary adjustments. Without a plan in place, I cannot make that assessment. Plans are not meant to be cast in concrete either. They serve as a guide when we are trying to reach a goal, and enable us to make better decisions when things come up that we did not anticipate.

There are always challenges that arise on just about every mission trip. They usually come from my own errors, a lack of knowledge, or cultural differences I was not aware of. These are things like bad cost estimates, miscommunication, or poor research, which are all human errors. And they are generally easy to resolve or correct.

But sometimes the challenges that arise are from God and His desire to accomplish His will and purpose. After all of these years of planning international mission trips I think I have finally learned how to recognize when it is God's intervention, and to adjust my plans accordingly. And I also know that if it is God's will, nothing I do will change His plan and purpose. I just need to follow His lead. Job acknowledged this when he said to God, *"I know that you can do all things; no plan of yours can be thwarted."* (**Job 42:2**) I simply need to recognize what Job did, and go where the Lord leads me and allow His purpose to supersede my plan.

One of the situations I sometimes face when I travel overseas is that the number of people who attend our training can differ dramatically from our estimate. Sometimes that is due to the overconfidence of our local host, but most of the time it is due to other local factors we were not aware of, such as holidays, other events in the area, and insufficient advertising. But whatever the reason, it is often disappointing to spend so much money and time to go and train somewhere, only to discover that very few pastors or leaders have shown up for the training. Fortunately, in my experience, it has generally been the exception rather than the rule. But on one such occasion I realized that it was God's purpose.

That occasion was in Belize in 2005. I had taken a mission team from a church in Knoxville, TN to go and do some construction, evangelism and training there. Several team members had put together some training based on Pastor Rick Warren's popular book, *The Purpose Driven Life*. It was to be an all-day conference and our host had invited people from many churches to attend the training. Our team was excited, and the trainers were prepared for the conference. But only one couple showed up for the training. Although we waited to see if more people would come, nobody did.

I gathered the team together and told them not to be disappointed. I did not blame our host or display any disappointment either. I simply reminded them that we were there on God's mission. Since we were prepared to train, we should go ahead and train these two people. I said I believed that God had a purpose that day, and we should just train and maybe we will find out what His purpose was later. We gathered for prayer and asked the Lord to bless and guide our training. We also asked Him to reveal His purpose to us.

So, we held the training conference as planned. We had a wonderful time of worship together and the trainers did a great job teaching what they had prepared. They also ministered to this one young couple who had come to the conference. The Holy Spirit was definitely working through the trainers that day!

At the end of the day, we had time to talk to this couple and hear their story and what brought them to the conference. We learned that they were an American missionary couple that had been ministering in Belize for several years but had recently come into a dry time. They began to question why they were there and what God's plan for them was. They were in a spiritual wilderness, struggling to understand their situation. They then shared that the conference was like an oasis in the desert for them. Our worship and training had refreshed their souls and given them a new perspective on their ministry in Belize.

You see, God had a purpose in mind when only two people came. It was the two people He felt needed to hear from His Spirit through our team. God used us to minister to the broken spirit of two missionaries whose only desire was to serve God in Belize. Because there were only two of them attending, the training became very personal and addressed the needs of this couple specifically. This likely would never have happened if we had 30 people in attendance. They might have been lost in the crowd and not had the opportunity to open up to the trainers as much as they did.

Our plan was to train 30 leaders in Belize. God's purpose was to refresh one couple. Our team now understood why they were there that day, and they were so blessed by it. It was a wonderful spiritual learning experience! God also answered our prayer that morning by revealing His purpose to us.

I had another experience where God's purpose overtook my plans. It was in Peru two years later with another team from the same church in Knoxville, TN. On this particular mission trip, we were going to the city of Trujillo to do construction, evangelism and children's ministry (VBS). Our host was David Quispirroca, a Peruvian pastor who I knew well and had worked with on several trips to Peru before.

David had made all of the local contacts and set up our ministry for the three days we would spend there. We had planned to work with three churches in Trujillo, and would spend a day with each church doing all three activities mentioned above. We had planned to divide up the team when we got to each location as needed. By this time, I had led mission teams for about eight years and felt pretty comfortable with our planning and with David as our host. What could go wrong? It did not take long to find out!

We first arrived in Lima and took a train up to Trujillo the next day. We checked into our hotel late in the afternoon, had dinner, and then met with our local hosts for a briefing meeting that night at our hotel to confirm all of our ministry plans for the next three days. When we got to the meeting room, there were already a lot of people there, more than what we would have expected from the three churches we had planned on working with.

We quickly discovered that word had gotten out about our mission team coming to Trujillo and other churches in the community wanted us to come and serve them as well. Consequently, there were pastors and leaders from 21 churches at the meeting that all wanted us to serve and minister in each of their churches!

At that moment I realized that the plans we had made had suddenly been "thrown out the window," as we Americans often say. I was also not in a position to negotiate what our team could do with 21 different churches. It was beyond my capability at that time because of my limited Spanish speaking ability.

So, I looked to my friend and local host, David, and said, "It looks like this is all in your hands now," referring to the fact that they were all speaking in Spanish and I was not able to communicate effectively enough to participate. Since I trusted David and his judgment, I told him to do the best he could to work out a new plan for our team. I left the outcome up to God and prayed for His Spirit to help David work out a new plan.

At the end of the meeting, David told me that he committed that our team would try to meet the needs of all of the 21 churches. We would have to split up the team each day into three groups and go to different churches and locations around the city for our various ministry activities. This meant that we now needed three buses and three team leaders (one for each group), and would have to coordinate our lunch breaks and other logistics. It was a very challenging commitment.

David and I gathered the team together and told them about the new plan. We then prayed for God's discernment and wisdom so that we could accomplish what was requested of us.

The next morning we got up early and met as a team before breakfast to come up with a strategy as to how we were going to do this. After praying for God's Spirit to guide us, we first had to determine how to split the team up into three groups. The team leader from the church in Knoxville, Mike, was chosen to determine who would do what each day. He divided the team into the three groups for that day – one for evangelism, one for construction, and one for VBS. Each group was assigned a team leader. Mike, Pastor Lane (the church pastor from Knoxville), and I were each chosen to go with one of the three groups to assist them as needed. Each group would visit seven churches for their specific ministry purpose and we would all meet for lunch together to have fellowship and discuss any issues.

We followed the same process each morning of the three days we spent in Trujillo. We would first meet to have our morning devotion and pray for God's wisdom and direction. Mike would then divide up the teams differently each day so that everyone would have an opportunity to participate in all three types of ministry. Then we would go out in three groups to visit seven churches.

What was so amazing about it all was seeing team members step forward and do ministry that they had not expected or prepared for, such as using puppets, swinging a hammer, or sharing the gospel with a local family. But at the end of each day, when we would gather for dinner, the stories of the day came out. There were so many testimonies of how God was using them in ways they never anticipated. God's Spirit was alive and active in all of our team members in Trujillo! It was really awesome and something that still gives me chills today when I recall that trip.

On top of all that, I never heard one complaint about the confusion, the last-minute changes, the daily grind, or the assignments they were given. They were all joyful and filled with the Holy Spirit, and ready to serve in whatever way God was asking them to minister that day. It was by far the most enjoyable mission team I have ever led. They were truly an inspiration to me and indicative of what a mission team should be all about – serving others in God's name and through God's Spirit! God had His purpose for this team despite our plans, and we were all so blessed to experience the joy and impact of letting go of our plans and letting God and His Spirit use us for His plan!

Whenever I work with local hosts there is always the possibility of miscommunication. Many times it has to do with cultural differences. Sometimes it has to do with language differences. Other times it has to do with technology problems, like internet access. I have attended several conferences to learn about working cross-culturally, yet I still don't always see things from their perspective. Although all of the local hosts I typically work with speak English, English is often not their native language. Consequently, sometimes there are words and phrases they may not understand as I do. And while the internet is a global tool, not everyone has the same access or skill with using it. As a result, plans can often go awry, and usually do.

One such time was when I went to Argentina in 2016 to do our Management for Church Leaders™ (MCL) training in the town of Quilmes, just outside Buenos Aires. I had been to Quilmes a few years earlier to train with the same host, Pastor Jorge, so I already knew him and the city fairly well. However, on this occasion I was communicating with Pastor Jorge directly in Spanish. I do speak and read Spanish, but I am not fluent. However, with my Spanish skills and translator apps on the internet, I felt I could handle organizing this second trip with him without an interpreter.

So, he and I emailed back and forth in Spanish, and I sent him training materials and information about organizing our training conference for this trip. He was already familiar with this process from our previous training. We agreed on the logistics, training venue (which was different than the first time), and schedules. He agreed to take responsibility for printing the training materials for our training, arranging our local transportation, and providing our lodging in Quilmes.

On this particular trip I was bringing a new training partner with me, someone whom I had met once or twice but did not know extremely well. His name was Samuel Quispirroca. And yes, he was David's brother from Cusco, Peru. He was also a pastor and a Bible school teacher and spoke some English. He previously had attended our MCL training years earlier in Peru and he was familiar with it. I sent him the training materials and the Trainer's manual in English for him to teach from, and told him to use them to prepare for his teaching

His English was as good as my Spanish, so we made a great team! Often times when we would communicate, he would ask me something in Spanish and I would reply in Spanish until I ran out of words and then switch to English. He would then respond to me in English until he ran out of English words and go back to Spanish. It was hilarious but effective. Even in our communication the Holy Spirit was helping us!

We first met up at our lodging in Quilmes. They had arranged for us to use an apartment which they provided to visiting teachers and missionaries. We arrived separately but had no trouble getting in to the apartment or getting settled in.

Later that afternoon, our local host came to the apartment to discuss the training with both of us, which was to begin the next evening. At that meeting he gave me a copy of the training manual in Spanish that he had printed, and everything looked great and ready to go. We had the next day to ourselves to rest and get ready, and he said he would come back the next afternoon around 5 pm to pick us up for the training that night.

After he left, Samuel and I went out to a nearby restaurant for dinner. During the course of our dinner conversation, he asked me if I had noticed that the training manual our host had printed for the conference was for our 2nd volume of our MCL training. I said no. I was surprised because I had planned to teach our 1st volume, the same one I taught the last time I was in Quilmes (to a different group of leaders). That was also the training I had sent to Samuel to prepare for. When we got back to our apartment, he showed me the printed training manual in Spanish and sure enough, it was our MCL Volume #2 training manual. I suddenly realized we had prepared for the wrong training!

The good news was that we had the entire next day to figure out what to do before the training started that night. Typically we train during the day. But because the pastors and leaders in Quilmes were bi-vocational and worked during the day, we had to hold our training at night (our schedule was to train from 6:30 – 10:30 pm for four nights). I had learned long ago to be prepared for anything, and I had copies of all of our training manuals on my laptop computer. All I needed to do was to download a copy of our MCL Volume #2 Trainer manual to a flash drive and find a place to print a copy for each of us to teach from.

So, the next morning we scoured the local area and found a print shop that was able to print the document for us from my flash drive. Once printed, we took the two copies back to our apartment and each began to make notes and prepare for our training that week.

We taught the training that they had anticipated, and it went very well. We never told them that we had prepared for the other training either. As a matter of fact, there were chapters from the MCL Volume #2 training that seemed to be particularly effective and meaningful for them. As a result, we had great interaction and participation from the attendees. It seemed that this training was just what they needed at this time in their city and ministries. It then became obvious to me–that was God's purpose!

I would also like to add three more points to this story. First, God had already given me the foresight to be prepared for something like this. His Spirit had led me to think through everything I might need for a trip and to bring copies just in case. Second, God arranged it so that we would have an entire day to make the changes necessary for this different training. He already knew we would need that time to prepare before the training started that night. Third, God's Spirit allowed us the opportunity to better prepare for this training since Samuel and I were together in the same place. We had such good discussion during our preparation time that really helped both of us become better trainers for the people there. Obviously, God knew what these people needed and His Spirit arranged it so that, through us, His purpose would be accomplished!

One final instance when God's purpose prevailed was also quite dramatic. On a trip to Liberia in 2012, my local host, a pastor whom I had met twice in Africa and once in the USA, abandoned me at a hotel the morning after my arrival. I was there to train at a training conference in Monrovia that he was to arrange. He did not return for lunch as he had promised, and he had also given me an incorrect cell phone number so that I could not contact him. I was betrayed by the one person I least expected since I knew him well, or at least thought I did! He essentially left me there to fend for myself. He had also pocketed the money I had given him for our training conference expenses ($800 for printing training materials and providing food for the participants). This is the only time I have been scammed or misled in my 20 years of organizing training conferences in the mission field.

I was now stuck in Liberia for seven days since my flight only flew there once a week. With no training conference to teach at, I prayed about what I should do. God's Spirit reminded me that I had another contact in Liberia who was a pastor that I had met through email. I had his contact information on my laptop that I brought with me. So, I dialed his phone number on my cell phone and he answered right away. It turned out he lived five minutes from my hotel!

He came right over, and I told him my story. He felt bad for me and my situation. I asked if I could perhaps teach his church leaders since I had nothing else to do there. He said to give him some time that afternoon and he would try to set up a training conference for me at his church.

He called me back that night and said he could muster eight of his church leaders for a training conference the next day. I was thrilled and said that was great! I went to bed happy that night that I would at least be able to train someone and not have to waste my time in Liberia. I thanked the Lord for providing this opportunity to still train some leaders there. His Spirit had been with me as well, helping me to overcome this situation.

When I arrived at his church the next morning, I was surprised to see that there were 35 pastors and leaders there, some of whom traveled several hours to get there! Once again, God had a purpose for my trip to Liberia despite what my original host had done. It was not what I had planned, but it turned out even better than what I had planned! It reminded me of the story of Joseph and his brothers in the Bible. Joseph said to them, *"You intended to harm me, but God intended it for good to accomplish what is now being done, the saving of many lives."* (**Genesis 50:20**) God's purpose once again proved better than my plan!

It is so easy for us to limit what God and the power of His Spirit can do. What seems impossible for us is never too hard for Him. Jesus reminds us of this when he said, *"With man this is impossible, but with God, all things are possible."* (**Matthew 19:26**) These experiences served to remind me that God is in control. He is sovereign, and He will bring about His purpose, in His time, and by His Spirit.

Will that stop me from planning? No, because God's Spirit still guides our plans as a means of preparing us for the work that He has called us to do for Him. But God has also taught me to trust in Him and His purposes and not my plans. His Word reminds all of us to *"Trust in the Lord with all your heart and lean not on your own understanding. Acknowledge Him in all your ways and He will make your paths straight."* (**Proverbs 3:5-6**)

As you reflect on your life, have you experienced times when God brought about his purpose instead of yours? Did that excite you or disappoint you? Were you able to recognize God's bigger plan, or did that leave you confused and frustrated because of all the planning and hard work you had put forth for another purpose? Did that kind of experience lead you to stop planning or working towards an important goal of yours?

It is my hope that it did not. I pray that you can realize, as I did, that God is sovereign and the one in control. God has the right, and the prerogative, to bring about His purpose through His children as He desires. We are made in His image and we must seek to align our will with His. When we accept that truth and submit ourselves to Him in obedience and humility, God will use us to bring about His purpose in our lives and the lives of others. It is an incredible blessing when we learn the spiritual lesson that God's purpose prevails!

Chapter 4

LESSON #2: GOD IS ALWAYS AT WORK

"He will not let your foot slip – He who watches over you will not slumber; indeed He who watches over you will neither slumber nor sleep."
Psalm 121:3-4

I have often wondered what people think God does all day. I suspect that some think He is always busy helping other people in very serious situations and does not have time for their insignificant problems. Others, I suspect, may think God is like the Maytag repairman from the television commercials of the past. The commercial was making the point that Maytag appliances were so reliable and dependable that their repairman had nothing to do. They just sat around all day waiting for a service call which never came. Perhaps people think God is just sitting up in heaven on his throne taking a nap or waiting for someone to send up a prayer so that He has something to do. Many Christians believe that God is reliable and dependable, but only when He is called upon to do something. The point is that we don't always think that God is at work, especially if we don't have any crisis or need for Him to act on our behalf.

The truth is that God and His Spirit are always at work, whether we know it or not. As humans we tend to only take into consideration the things that we see or know of. We make assumptions that are based on information or knowledge that we can see, read or hear about. But the reality is that there are always things going on behind the scenes that we might not be aware of. Maybe it's a surprise birthday party someone has planned for us. Maybe it's a boss working with someone in Human Resources to get us a job promotion. Or maybe it's an identity thief using our identity to take out a mortgage in our name or steal from our bank account. Just because we don't know about these things, or see them, does not mean they aren't taking place.

In a similar fashion, God is always working behind the scenes whether we know it or not. But we must also recognize that God's Spirit is always working for our good and never to harm us in any way. The Apostle Paul says, *"And we know that in all things God works for the good of those who love him, who have been called according to His purpose."* (**Romans 8:28**) God is sovereign and always working His will for mankind. Much of the work He does is beyond our ability to see or know. Faith in God means to put our trust in Him and to know that His Spirit is working out _all_ things for our spiritual benefit, not just those things we can see.

My first experience in seeing how God was always at work came from a mission trip to the Philippines in August of 1997. My wife and I were part of a team of 14 people, most of whom were members of a church from Charlotte, NC. Their church had been organizing annual mission trips to do worship ministry training in other nations, and they also invited others to join them. This was our second mission trip with them, having been part of a team that went to Almaty, Kazakhstan to do a worship conference the previous year. Kim and I both taught workshops on this trip and I also played guitar in the praise band at the conference. After we arrived in Manila, we spent a couple of days there getting acclimated to the climate and the time change. We also had some time to visit the city.

Since our worship conference was to take place in the town of Tabuk in the northern part of the island of Luzon, we went to the local airport for our flight up to the city of Tuguegerao, the nearest city to Tabuk with an airport. When we arrived at the counter to check-in for the flight, the ticket agent told us that we did not have confirmed seats on the flight. Apparently, back in those days and unknown to us, our trip leader was required to call the local airline the day before to confirm our seats on the flight. He had failed to do that and so they gave up our confirmed seats to others. Since that was the only flight that day, we were in a bit of a dilemma. The airplane was not very big (perhaps 60 seats in total), and so the chance of getting 14 available seats was not very good at that late time.

We began to discuss what to do. The first thing we decided to do was to pray that we could still get on that flight. After praying, one of the team members suggested that while we waited our dance team could practice one of their dance routines to help pass the time. As they began to dance, the rest of us sang and worshiped the Lord. Soon thereafter the other passengers in the terminal area gathered around and began to worship right along with us. It was an incredible impromptu time of worship in an airline terminal!

After our dance team had finished the dance, the airline manager behind the counter called our team leader up to the counter. He told him that he was a Christian too and would do his best to hold some seats for us. He said some of the passengers might not show up, but he could not guarantee he could get all 14 seats. So, we resumed praying and asking the Lord to make 14 seats available for our team to be able to fly up together to Tugueguerao that afternoon.

As the closing time for check-in drew near, the airline manager came on the loudspeaker and informed us (and everyone in the terminal) that there were exactly 14 unclaimed seats on the flight and that he could check-in our entire team now. The terminal erupted with applause and a chorus of Amen! God had done what we thought might be impossible!

What this experience showed us was that God's Spirit was working behind the scenes to ensure our team would be able to go where He had sent us. It was His purpose and plan and He would make a way. We do not know all the little circumstances and situations that God had orchestrated to get our team on the plane. That's not important. What is important is that His Spirit was working the entire time to bring about His will. We will never know who the 14 people were that did not show up for the flight that day. But we do know someone who did show up – God!

Two years later I had a more personal experience of seeing how God was working in the background. It was on the very first mission team I led through an organization called Missions International. I had gone on four of their mission trips and after returning from the trip to the Philippines in 1997 (as mentioned above), I felt the call to recruit and lead a team from our church in Chicago to go and do children and youth ministry training. My wife was our church's part time children's ministry leader at that time, and we had just hired a new youth minister who had always wanted to go on a mission trip. It seemed like a good fit for our church.

So, in the fall of 1997 I recruited a mission team from our church, and we met together in our home to decide where we should go. Missions International suggested to me that we should go to Peru as this type of training would be very helpful for the churches there. They had a very good contact and host for us in that country as well. As our team prayed over several possibilities (Philippines, Kazakhstan, South Africa, and Peru), we gathered around a globe that still sits in my office today. We spun the globe and asked one of the team members to close their eyes and put their finger on it and stop the globe. Their finger landed right on Peru! We all agreed that this was a sign from the Lord that we should go to Peru.

Having never been to Peru and not knowing our host, I felt that it was important for me to go to Peru prior to our trip to meet this individual and get to know him. As it turns out, Missions International had a team going to Peru the next summer (June 1998) which was being hosted by this person. So, I was invited to go along on this mission trip to meet him and get a better understanding of Peru and its people.

Our host was a young pastor named David Quispirroca, who I mentioned earlier. He was involved with a ministry called DAWN 2000 (Discipling A Whole Nation), and had been active hosting mission teams all over Peru for that ministry. On this trip we ministered in the two largest cities in Peru, Lima and Cusco. This gave me an opportunity to learn about the

Peruvian culture and to better prepare me for leading a mission team there myself.

At the end of the trip, David suggested that for our trip we do the children and youth ministry training in Lima and a town called Juliaca. He also suggested that we come back the following January for that purpose.

When I got back from Peru and shared the experience of my trip and the locations David suggested for us with our mission team, they readily agreed to the plan to go there and train in January of 1999. It was now time to organize the trip and put that plan into motion!

At that time, my wife and I were also planning to move to Alpharetta, GA. She had recently been hired as the full-time Children's Minister at Christ the Shepherd Lutheran Church (where we still worship today), and was to start her new job at the end of July of 1998. Consequently, we were in the process of selling our home, which had not been going as well as we had hoped it would.

While I was in Peru on the exploratory mission trip, interested buyers moving back from Japan expressed an interest in our home and submitted an offer. However, they had their possessions already coming back to the USA so they wanted to close fairly soon so they could move their things right into a new home rather than having to put them in storage. That was fine with us because we also wanted to close soon so we could move right away to Georgia.

So, right after I got home from Peru we negotiated the sale of our home to them with a closing date only a few weeks away. We then hopped into our car with our two children and drove to Alpharetta to find a new home for us there. We quickly found a home near our church in Alpharetta and were able to make an offer and have it accepted right away. We were also able to coordinate our closing in a few weeks as well because the home was not occupied. So, in late July of 1998, we moved to Georgia (although God was at work in our home move, this is not the point of this story).

With our move to Georgia the mission team started to change. We had about 12 people planning to go from our church in Illinois, but after leaving for Georgia several people decided not to go on the trip. Only three people from our former church remained committed to going to Peru, so I had to start recruiting other people to be part of our mission team. Since our trip to Peru was only five months away, I needed to act quickly.

At our new church in Georgia we found three people that were interested in going with us, including our ten-year-old son. We were able to add another four people from a church in El Cajon, CA that was now pastored by one of our former pastors from our Chicago church where we had moved from. We were also contacted by a youth minister from Kansas City who was interested in a mission trip for youth or children's ministry training. She joined the team as well. We also added a woman from the church in Knoxville, TN that I mentioned earlier.

In the end, we had a mission team of 14 people from different parts of the USA. They were all recruited in less than two months and most of them did not know each other! Several did not know me either! What started out as a desire to take a team to the mission field from our church in Chicago morphed into a conglomeration of people and backgrounds from multiple churches in different States. It would require more organization, preparation, and planning on my part since we were not all coming from the same place. That was definitely not in my original plan!

One of the challenges was arranging all of our flights from different cities. We were able to book flights on Continental airlines (now part of United) that all connected in Houston. So, we all met in Houston for the first time and flew to Peru from there. Having everyone arrive in time to make the flight to Peru was a small miracle in itself. It also showed us that God was at work even in our flight plans!

We had a wonderful conference in Lima. I had brought a guitar and led worship at the conference. My son accompanied me on the drums. I spent most of my time managing the team and making sure everyone had an opportunity to participate and serve. Some members of the team taught while others assisted or prayed. We came together as a team and were able to minister effectively to the children and youth ministry leaders that attended our training.

Our next stop was the city of Juliaca, which is high up in the Andes Mountains at about 12,500 feet. That's almost as high as Pikes Peak in Colorado (14,000 feet)! We had some difficulty adjusting to the altitude at first, but fortunately the Lord took care of us. Some team members had brought some altitude medication while others just needed some time to adjust. But by the next morning we were ready to head to the conference, which we were told was to be in an old farmhouse out in the country.

When we landed at the airport by Juliaca, the guitar was not in the baggage area as expected. Since we were meeting at a farmhouse out in the country, I felt that the guitar was essential for me to be able to lead worship. I then began to be concerned about not having an instrument for worship, which was an important part of our training conferences. When I inquired with the airline about the guitar, they said it was accidentally put back on the plane and flown back to Lima. They said they could have it to me the next afternoon. Unfortunately, I needed it to start our conference the next morning. So, I started praying about what to do for worship without a guitar.

As we drove on the bus to the old farmhouse the next morning, I was still uncertain about what to do about worship. I continued to pray for an answer from the Lord. But I was not getting an answer. So I just figured we would have to have worship with no instruments and sing acapella. It wasn't my preference, but it would have to do.

When we arrived at the farmhouse I thought I heard music coming from within. As I walked inside, I saw a full praise band with electric guitars, bass guitar, drums and vocalists! I was stunned! I had assumed there would be no electricity and never thought they would have a praise band already prepared. But you know what? God knew! Because God was already at work through the Holy Spirit!

I knew right then that God was behind every aspect of our mission trip making it happen! His Holy Spirit was at work even when I did not know it. He was preparing the hearts of those who would go with us to train and serve. He was orchestrating the many different flights and resources we would need. He was making sure all of us arrived in Houston on time so we could fly together as a team. He was preparing the praise team to lead worship at our conference. And I could go on and on listing the many ways the Holy Spirit was at work before, during and after our trip to Peru. And that knowledge helped me so much in leading mission teams in the future all over the globe!

I would like to add one final, short story from a different perspective. It is about how God might be at work in our ministry in ways we do not see.

I had the wonderful opportunity to go and train in China in 2015. By this time, I was no longer leading mission teams but entirely focused on taking our Management for Church Leaders training to 100 nations around the world. We had a wonderful host in China who had arranged for us to train in both Shanghai and Beijing. However, we did not find out where we were training, or what hotel we would be staying at, until about three days before we left the USA. At the time I thought this was a bit unusual. But I deferred to our host on this matter and did not question it.

Our first conference was in Shanghai and was held at a large Chinese University a few blocks away from our hotel. In fact, we were meeting in a classroom in the Business School building. I subsequently learned that the Head of the Business School was a Christian, and the conference was advertised at the last minute so as not to arouse the interest of their government, although it had been planned to be held there for months. I was also surprised to learn that there were going to be non-Christians attending the training who were business professionals and not church leaders or pastors. The same was true at our training conference in Beijing.

Even though our training was filled with Scriptural references and Biblical examples, we were free to share them, and our Christian faith, in our teaching. This was something I would not have expected in China. When I asked our host about why this was the case, she told us that the Chinese love to learn about leadership and management, especially from Americans. It did not matter to the participants that it was Biblically based.

So, despite China being a communist nation, we had the opportunity to share our training, as well as the gospel and God's Word, with non-Christian business professionals! God was at work the whole time we were planning and getting ready for the trip, and His Holy Spirit was preparing those business leaders to hear His Word through our training! We did not even think about that or consider that this could ever be a possibility until we arrived at the training conference in Shanghai. You can imagine our surprise and joy in being used by God for His greater purpose!

It is likely that God has also been at work behind the scenes throughout your life. Have you witnessed His Spirit bring about a change in a friend or family member? Have you experienced a blessing that you believe came about because of God's intervention? Have you seen circumstances change in a miraculous way that amazed you? Were you aware at the time that it was God at work, or did you just chalk it up to fate or coincidence? With God there is no coincidence. God often works in ways we can't see and He is purposeful and intentional in what He does (**Philippians 2:13**).

It is my hope that you will take the time to reflect on those situations that happened in your past that perhaps God had orchestrated for your benefit. It could have been a miraculous healing. Maybe it was a set of circumstances that all came together at just the right time to make something wonderful happen for you. Perhaps it was a job opportunity that seemed to come out of nowhere right after you lost a job. Whatever it was, if you look back, you will be able to recognize how God was at work in those situations. Then you will know and understand that God is constantly at work in our world, and in your life and mine, to accomplish what He desires.

Yes, God and His Holy Spirit are always at work even when we aren't. He works His will through all situations according to His purpose and plan. It may be arranging transportation, providing for worship music, or preparing people to hear his Word as I experienced. Or maybe you experienced God at work in different ways in your life. Whatever is necessary, God will accomplish it! As the word of God proclaims, *"So is my word that goes out from my mouth: it will not return to me empty but will accomplish what I desire and achieve the purpose for which I sent it."* **(Isaiah 55:11)**

Chapter 5

LESSON #3: GOD HEARS OUR PRAYERS

"Is any one of you is in trouble? He should pray."
James 5:13

The prayer life of a Christian is their lifeline to God. It is the method that Jesus taught us to communicate with our Heavenly Father and to *"put our hope in God, who richly provides us with everything for our enjoyment."* (**1Timothy 6:17**) My prayer life has expanded greatly over the years, mostly from my growth in faith and trying to be obedient to God's Word.

Growing up, my prayers tended to be private and personal. They were only in my head or my heart. Most people in the church I grew up in did not pray out loud or to others, and neither did my parents. It took me a long time to be able to learn to pray publicly. As a matter of fact, it was my biggest fear on my first international mission trip to Kazakhstan. It was on that trip that the Holy Spirit showed me how to pray more publicly. And since that time, I have grown in my prayer life and my ability to pray for others and in public.

I also learned on that first trip that when one is in the mission field, and in a foreign nation, prayer becomes very important. Everything we do on a mission trip is for the Lord. So, it is imperative that we call upon the Holy Spirit to seek His wisdom, direction, protection and provision since He is the one who sent us there! We also often find ourselves in situations we may be unfamiliar with or unable to understand due to the cultural and language differences.

Prayer enables us to call on God for help, anytime and anywhere! Even when Moses was leading the Israelites through the desert to the Promised Land, He relied on the Lord to lead and guide them. He did not rely on his own strength or knowledge, but instead prayed to the Lord for help throughout their journey.

Prayer is perhaps the most important tool we have as Christians. Not just for mission trips, but also for everyday life. God is available 24 hours a day, 7 days a week and 365 days a year. His line is always open and He is waiting to take our call. We never get a busy signal and we will never be put on hold.

We also don't have to navigate a menu of selections of what we want to talk to Him about before He listens. Once we call upon the Holy Spirit, we have direct and immediate access. No question is too dumb. No request is too large. And no hurt is too trivial. God listens to the outpourings of our heart. His Word tells us, ***"This is the confidence we have in approaching God: that if we ask anything according to his will, He hears us."*** **(1 John 5:14)**

God responds to our prayers as well in several ways.

First, He longs to give us His wisdom. ***"If any of you lacks wisdom, he should ask God, who gives*** *generously to all without finding fault, and it will be given to him."* (**James 1:5**)

Second, God wants to give us His protection. God protected Shadrach, Meshach and Abednego in the blazing furnace. They told King Nebuchadnezzar, *"If we are thrown into the blazing furnace, the God we serve is able to save us from it, and He will rescue us from your hand."* (**Daniel 3:17**)

Third, God promises us His help in our time of need. *"I lift up my eyes to the hills–where does my help come from? My help comes from the Lord, the Maker of heaven and earth."* (**Psalm 121:1-2**)

Finally, God gives us His compassion. *"The Lord is good to all; he has compassion on all he has made."* (**Psalm 145:9**)

Even when words fail us, God already knows what is in our heart. Solomon prayed to the Lord saying that He alone knows the hearts of men. Solomon said, *"Forgive and act: deal with each man according to all he does, since you know his heart (for you alone know the hearts of all men)."* (**1 Kings 8:39**) We also know from Scripture that His Holy Spirit intercedes for us. *"In the same way, the Spirit helps us in our weakness. We do not know what we ought to pray for, but the Spirit himself intercedes for us with groans that words cannot express."* (**Romans 8:26**)

While His answers may not always be immediate, they will always be perfectly timed! He gives us what we need, when we need it, and in a manner that is the most beneficial for us. His objective is always to bring about His will and purpose for our lives. The Bible reminds us that *"...it is God who works in you to will and act according to His good purpose."* (**Philippians 2:13**)

Prayer has been important in my daily life and has helped me to overcome illness, tragedy, loss, fear and failure. I have experienced the power of prayer more profoundly, however, while on international mission trips. I believe it is because I am in a foreign country and away from home and what is familiar to me.

But it is also the nature of mission trips that brings Satan to the forefront. He wants to destroy me and my relationship with Jesus because I go in His name. He wants to thwart my activities on God's behalf. He wants to silence me so that I cannot share God's Word with others. And he will do anything to stop me if I am being effective for the Lord. Whenever we go to serve others in God's name, Satan is not happy and he *"prowls around like a roaring lion looking for someone to devour."* (**1 Peter 5:8**).

It is not surprising, then, that I have experienced the attacks of Satan while on many mission trips. Sometimes they are simply obstacles to work around. Sometimes they are an attempt to stop me completely from doing what I am doing. Other times they generate fear or concern that causes me to hesitate or lack the courage I need. Whatever the attack, they are always designed to draw me away from God and to fill me with doubt and anxiety.

Prayer is the antidote to Satan and his attacks. Prayer is the means by which we can get around Satan's obstacles, keep going and not stop, and overcome our fears and doubts. To put it simply, without prayer, Satan wins. God's Word tells us, *"Submit yourselves, then, to God. Resist the devil, and he will flee from you."* (**James 4:7**) When we call on Jesus in prayer, Satan will flee!

One of the most difficult situations that I have ever encountered as a mission trip leader happened in Peru in 2005. It was the very first time that I had been out of my country longer than two weeks. I was leading mission trips in those years and had three teams that all wanted to go to Peru that summer. So, I decided to arrange them all as back to back trips so that I would only have to buy one airline ticket and thus save money on my airfare. The plan was that I would stay down in Peru for a month while each team came and went.

Because of that decision, there was a lot more planning and coordination needed to organize three separate trips. I was also dealing with three separate team leaders from three different locations in the USA, and I needed to arrange the travel so that as one team left the next team came. It also had to be done without any overlap between trips so that I could devote my full attention to each team. I prayed very hard for these trips and that the Holy Spirit would guide me in my planning and leadership.

With the Lord's help the planning went very well. His Holy Spirit helped me to organize the flights for each team to arrive and then leave right around the time the next team showed up. In addition to booking the flights, the plans also included booking hotels, arranging all of the team meetings, preparing the materials for each team (luggage tags, team shirts, team handbooks, forms and other information), and coordinating internal transportation, ministry activities and meals with our local hosts.

For the first team I worked with a local host in Peru, David Quispirroca, whom I have already mentioned. He made all of the local arrangements for us. I personally made all of the arrangements for the second team, which happened to be just my wife and me. Our local hosts in Peru were two missionary couples, one from

America and one from Argentina, both of whom I knew and had met on previous trips to Peru. The third team had made all of their local arrangements with their own contact in Peru for their ministry work.

God heard my prayers for all of the needed logistics for the three groups that I was responsible for coordinating, and the plans all came together!

The first group, a 17 member youth ministry team from Kansas City comprised of both youth and adults, came to Peru to minister in the cities of Arequipa and Paucartambo. As we gathered for our first team meeting, we prayed that God would use us for His glory in Peru. In Arequipa, the team first went to different plazas for street evangelism, singing songs, doing dramas and sharing testimonies. While the songs and dramas generated interest, it was the testimonies of the youth from the team that drew the attention of the local Peruvians. We saw many of them step forward to receive Christ!

The team also found time to interact with local youth through sports ministry, playing soccer, kick ball, and volleyball at a local park. They also shared their testimonies with the Peruvian youth. God heard our prayers, and He used the team to witness to their faith and draw new believers to Him!

We then flew to Cusco and took a bus up into the Andes, to a village called Paucartambo. We were invited to lead a three day Christian youth camp for 100 local youth there. The lodging they provided for us had no heat, no hot water, and no showers, and the bathrooms were atrocious and unsanitary. The temperature at night would get down to below freezing, so it was very cold as well.

The conditions were very hard on the team, especially the women and young girls. Several of our team members got sick. But through our prayers, the Holy Spirit helped us make it through the three days we spent there. Consequently, we had an enjoyable and effective time of ministry in both cities, despite the difficulties. God indeed heard our prayers!

The team flew back to Lima and headed home to the USA. As I saw them off at the airport, my wife, Kim, flew in for the second mission trip. She and I were there to do children's ministry training conferences in the cities of Ayacucho and Cusco. As always, we prayed for good health, safe travel and effective training.

We first went to Ayacucho where we were hosted by American missionaries I had previously met there. They also hosted Kim and me in their home. Unfortunately, on the first day of training, I got very sick with flu like symptoms, which I attributed to my time in Paucartambo. I was so weak that I was unable to assist Kim with any training and slept most of the time in the church while she taught. I prayed for God to give her the strength to do the training all by herself and to heal me quickly. God heard my prayers and He responded! She was able to do all of the training by herself and I felt much better by the time we left Ayacucho. The Holy Spirit strengthened both of us!

We then headed to Cusco to teach a children's ministry conference there. Our host was a missionary couple from Argentina I had met on my first trip to Peru. God blessed our training at their church as well and we had a wonderful time of ministry with some of the local children's ministry leaders. I was also able to participate and help with worship leading and some of the training. God had heard, and answered, our prayers and our trip was successful!

When we got back to Lima, I took Kim to the airport and sent her on her way. Afterwards, I went to the main plaza in Lima to meet the third team that had arrived from San Diego the day before.

This team was comprised of 18 adults, who had come to bring a ministry to Peru called Celebrate Recovery, a ministry started by Pastor Rick Warren and Saddleback Church. They also had an aggressive schedule of training in five cities over two weeks. Despite my being weary from the last 20 days in Peru and the illness I had, I knew that this team was well prepared and all I had to do was make sure I got the team from location to location. Unfortunately, it was not going to be that easy.

The trip started out well with our first training conference in Lima. The team did a great job teaching the Celebrate Recovery ministry there. Everyone was in a joyful mood as we headed by overnight bus to our second location, the city of Trujillo. The two days of training there went well also and we took an overnight bus back to Lima. We then headed straight to the airport to fly to our third destination, the city of Arequipa. The training conference there was also successful, and so far we were blessed that everything was going according to plan. Three conferences done and two more to go!

When we arrived at the airport in Arequipa for our flight to Cusco, we were informed by the airline that there was some sort of problem with the incoming flight and it was canceled. They told us that we were bumped to a flight the next day. However, because we had a training conference that began the next morning in Cusco we needed to get there that day. We pleaded with the airline, LanPeru, but to no avail. They offered to put us all on an overnight bus to Cusco, and so we decided to take that option in order to not have to delay our training conference the next day.

So, we went back to the city and waited for the nighttime bus to Cusco. While the team explored more of Arequipa, I went to the LanPeru office to make sure we had tickets on the flight from Cusco to Puerto Maldonado three days later. They assured us we were booked on the flight and so I felt relieved that this was just a one day problem. I silently thanked God for that answered prayer.

We made it to Cusco early enough the next morning and were able to start our training conference on-time. Although the team was pretty tired from the overnight bus ride they did not complain. We were all happy just to be there to train as planned!

When we arrived at the airport in Cusco a couple of days later for our flight to our final destination, Puerto Maldonado, we were told that we did not have any seat assignments on the flight and were being bumped to the same flight the following day. I told the ticket agent that their office in Arequipa assured me we would be on the flight. She apologized and said there were no more seats left and we would have to wait until the next day's flight.

At this point there was no other option to get to Puerto Maldonado. This city was in the jungle and there were no buses that could take us there. So we were forced to spend an extra night in Cusco and cancel the first day of our training in Puerto Maldonado (this was the only time in my 24 years of mission trips that we ever had to cancel a day of a training!).

Although we were stuck in Cusco, we now had the opportunity to attend a concert by Marcos Witt, perhaps the most well-known Hispanic Worship Leader and

Songwriter. Marcos was a worship leader from Dallas, TX, but grew up as the son of German missionaries in Mexico. We had seen billboards and posters around Cusco about the concert, so we knew it was that night. We prayed that we could get rooms at the hotel we had previously stayed at for the night, and for all of us to get tickets for the concert as well. God came through for us once again on both of our requests!

So, we left the airport and went back to our hotel and checked in again. While the team rested at the hotel, I went to the LanPeru office in Cusco to inquire as to our flight status to Puerto Maldonado and also back to Lima. I was more concerned about our flight back to Lima because we all had to connect to our flights back to the USA. As a result, I asked them to give me our boarding passes now for that flight, as well as our flight to Puerto Maldonado the following day. LanPeru gave them to me and assured me we would all be on the flight back to Lima as scheduled. I felt so relieved that we would not miss our flight back to Lima and our connecting flights back home.

We thoroughly enjoyed the Marcos Witt concert that night. It was truly inspiring and uplifting. It also helped us all forget the difficulties we encountered getting to Cusco. An added benefit was having the opportunity to meet him the following morning at the airport in Cusco on our way to Puerto Maldonado. He was flying back to Dallas that day but was in the same gate area. It was a joy to meet him and to share with him our purpose in Peru and how much we enjoyed his concert.

Our flight to Puerto Maldonado the next morning had no issues. Despite having only one day of training in Puerto Maldonado, it went very well and was gratefully received by the people there. That night we celebrated what the Lord had accomplished through our team on this entire trip. We also thanked God for what He had done in us these past two weeks as well.

We got up the next morning and headed to the airport with our bags packed and our boarding passes to Lima in hand. When we got up to the check-in counter and handed the ticket agent our boarding passes, he said that all the available seats on the plane were taken. We were going to have to take the flight going to Lima the next day. When I explained that we all had connecting flight back to the USA to catch that night he said there was nothing he could do.

At this point, I was very frustrated and angry with LanPeru. I was so furious that they had lied to me because they had given me boarding passes they knew were no good. I know that because the agent in Puerto Maldonado said that their computer system is not on-line with the one in Cusco and they issue boarding passes only upon check-in. It was obvious to me that the LanPeru office in Cusco had to know that. Apparently, they just kept bumping passengers from one day to the next due to the cancelation of the initial flight. The airline just lied to my face over and over again to push the problem down the line to the next city.

For me, this was the last straw. I had finally reached my breaking point.

Realizing that the team was there along with our Peruvian hosts, I did not want to react in front of them or create an international incident. So, I just found a quiet corner of the airport terminal, sat down, and cried. There was nothing I could do. I was exhausted from my month-long journey and the many miles I had traveled. I was so frustrated by the airline and their lies. I was now going to have to deal with rearranging the flights of eighteen people back to the USA. I also did not know if we could go back to our hotel that we had stayed in, or where we might go if it wasn't available. All I could do was pray.

So, I poured out my heart, my frustration and my anger to the Lord. He listened and He heard me. I then felt the peace and calm of the His Spirit come over me and assure me that He would take care of us.

After perhaps 15 minutes of my sulking and prayers, I rejoined the team. They were all there seemingly unflustered by what was taking place. They were happy and just waiting to be told what the plan was. I looked over at the ticket counter and saw our Peruvian hosts still arguing with the LanPeru agents, begging for an explanation and to get us on the flight that day. But at that moment, I realized that whatever was happening was not in my control or anyone else's control. Yet it was still in God's hands! I turned everything over to Him, and tried to focus on serving the team and doing the best I could for them.

We left the airport and headed back to our hotel. God worked it out that we could extend our stay another night there. The team also now had some time to see the area and enjoy the local culture. Puerto Maldonado was in the jungle and a much different place than the other cities we had visited. I called our travel agent and she was able to cancel our flights back to the USA that night and book us all on flights the following night instead. She instructed me to talk to Continental Airlines when we got to the airport in Lima to finalize our re-bookings and get our boarding passes.

When we arrived in Lima the next morning, I sent the team on to see some of the sights of Lima while I spent the next few hours at the airport making sure all of our return flights to the USA were set for that night. Most of that time was spent haggling over who would pay for the new ticket cost. I was assured by LanPeru that they would pay the extra cost since our need to re-book our flights was their fault, but Continental Airlines was having a hard time confirming that with them. I was not surprised after what we had been through with LanPeru!

Although I was tired, I did not lose confidence that God would take care of everything. The Holy Spirit helped me to remain calm and just work through the situation. After some time, the two airlines were finally able to work it out. God did as I expected, and He enabled the entire team to fly home that night. It was a day late but at least we were all going home!

As you can see, this trip to Peru was quite extraordinary. I had to deal with all kinds of problems and situations that came up, and every time I called upon the Lord, He heard me and listened to me. He also answered our prayers and acted to accomplish His will for me as well as the teams I led. And although I have never flown LanPeru again, and probably won't, I learned the important lesson that God hears our prayers!

I have one additional experience to share about how God hears our prayers. It happened in Albania. I had organized a training of our Management for Church Leaders material in Korce, Albania and Thessaloniki, Greece in January of 2019. I had been to Albania twice before to train, but only in the capital city of Tirana, and both times in the summer month of May. Korce was a city up in the mountains and very different from the capital. It would also be winter and had the possibility of snow. I was also looking to forward to teaching in the city of Thessaloniki where the Apostle Paul taught and preached.

On the morning of our flight to Albania, my American training partner came down with the flu and could not go as planned to help me train. We talked about our options for him flying to meet up with us later, but none of them were workable. He did not know when he would be able to travel, and we would be going from place to place in Albania and Greece. As a result, it would be hard to plan where and when to meet him. Since this was at the very last minute, it was also hard to cancel or reschedule the trip.

I had been to Albania twice before and also knew our local host, Petrit, very well. As a result, I felt that in this situation I would be fine going on by myself. So, I prayed and asked the Lord for His guidance, and He indicated to me that I should go to Albania without my training partner. I was comfortable in going there alone and perhaps leaning on Petrit and others to help me train if needed. I felt at peace and that the Holy Spirit affirmed that decision.

When I arrived in Tirana, I finally informed Petrit that I did not have a training partner with me. He said that would not be a problem. As it turned out, we would not be alone either. Also joining us would be our van driver, his adult son, and a pastor from Korce (who set up our training there and who would accompany us to Greece). There was also going to be an American pastor from Georgia tagging along. He was there to get to know Albania and to minister in other ways on the trip. So, I ended being part of a team of six people! I now looked forward to seeing what God would do through all of us on this trip. I had my plans but obviously there were going to be changes!

Petrit and I were picked up by our van driver and his son in Tirana the next morning and then we headed to the local airport to pick up the American pastor who was arriving that day. After he arrived, the five of us first stopped for lunch near the airport, but also to add some better tires to the van due to the projected snowfall that night. Our driver wanted to make sure we would be safe driving through the mountains.

After that we started our journey up to Korce from Tirana. Along the way, we stopped for dinner part way up the mountain as daylight began to fade. When we came out of the restaurant, it was dark and had started to snow. The pavement was only wet, and so we continued our journey up the mountain. The road up the mountain was filled with hairpin turns and short straightaways, making the journey slow. The snow started coming down harder and began accumulating on the roadway, making it very slippery and dangerous. It was very dark and there were no lights on the road, except for those of the trucks, buses and vehicles trying to navigate the turns and steepness of the hill.

Pretty soon we began to see other vehicles having trouble getting up the hill and coming down the hill. It was very dangerous, but it seemed as though our van had good traction (thanks to the better tires they had installed), and we were able to continue. I started to get concerned and anxious about getting to Korce that night, and was hoping we would not get stranded on this mountain before reaching our destination. We had a training conference to start the next morning and I did not want to start this trip with a delay in our training, which could potentially impact the remainder of our trip. I also did not see any hotels or any other places where we could potentially stay along the road up the mountain.

As I sat in the backseat of the van, I just closed my eyes and began to pray fervently. I asked the Lord to give our driver good vision and steady hands to control the van, and I prayed that we could make it to Korce safely that night. I remained in prayer for the rest of our trip up the mountain in the snowstorm, which took about two hours. I was quite relieved when we got to the top of the mountain and the road leveled off.

When we arrived in the area around Korce, we found that it was covered with about a foot or more of snow. The main road was drivable due to the traffic, but the side roads were not. We were able to get close to the place where we were staying, but had to stop short due to the deep snow on the road. We got out of the van, collected our luggage, and walked a couple of blocks to get to our lodging, a home owned by an American missionary. Although I was cold and tired from the stress of the trip, I was thankful to be there.

They told us that while Korce does get snow, this storm was unusually heavy and a major blizzard! As a matter of fact, on our way back to Tirana through Korce, we drove on the same road going down the mountain, but this time during the day and with no snow on the road. As I looked out the window of the van, I was absolutely amazed at what the road looked like and wondered how we ever got up that mountain in that snowstorm. It was a miracle of God! God heard my prayers, and had brought us all safely to Korce!

I know God hears our prayers because I have witnessed it first-hand. He is not distant, nor absent, but is patiently waiting for us to pour out our heart to Him or seek His help. The Bible tells us, *"Does*

He who implanted the ear not hear?" (**Psalm 94:9**)
Indeed He does!

I would imagine that you too have experienced God's answer to prayer in your life. Maybe it was a difficult family situation, a problem at work, or a particular trying time that you were going through. As you think back on those occasions, did God answer your prayer? Did you receive the answer you wanted? Did God answer the prayer in a way that was more than you asked for? Did God answer you at all?

Many times God answers our prayers in ways we don't understand or don't like. Sometimes we don't get any answer at all. But that does not mean that God doesn't hear our prayers. It only means that we weren't really asking for His will to be done but ours instead. God will only do what is in accordance with His will, and sometimes that may not match what we desire to see happen. I would encourage you to pray for God's will as well as the answer that you want. But then trust in Him to do what is best. If we can all do that, we will not only learn that God answers our prayers, but we will also learn to accept God's answer and align ourselves with His will.

Chapter 6

LESSON #4: GOD CHOOSES US

> *"You did not choose me, but I chose you*
> *and appointed you to go and bear fruit –*
> *fruit that will last. Then the Father will give*
> *you whatever you ask in my name."*
> ***John 15:16***

All of us have experienced being chosen for something. Perhaps it was to participate in a game of some kind, to be on a sports team, to play in a band or orchestra, to portray a drama character in a skit or play, to win an award, to sing a solo, or to fill a job position. Whatever it was, it was always a great feeling to be chosen. I am equally sure that we have also experienced not being chosen. Perhaps you were left off the basketball team, failed a musical audition, or saw someone else get the job that you wanted. For many of us, the most painful experience was likely as a child on the school playground and not being chosen to be on either team. We would have to endure the shame of "not being good enough" to play in the game.

As human beings, one of our greatest needs is to belong and to participate with others. We don't want to be left out or feel as if we are not good enough to participate. That creates both a sense of loneliness and worthlessness that can scar our emotions and self-identity. Part of our sinful nature is trying to measure up to the standards of society or others. When we do that, it causes us to envy what we don't have, pity ourselves, or trample over others in our attempt to justify ourselves. These are all behaviors that end up destroying what we were created to be by God.

The good news is that we are all chosen by God. He doesn't leave anyone on the sidelines. Every believer is offered the opportunity to belong and participate. God's Word says, *"For every living soul belongs to me, the father as well as the son – both alike belong to me."* (**Ezekiel 18:4**) We all belong in the game! He does not consider anyone to be worthless or not good enough. He has gifted every person and desires that they use their gifts to serve others. As the Bible says, *"Each one should use whatever gift he has received to serve others, faithfully administering God's grace in its various forms."* (**1 Peter 4:10**)

God also has a purpose for all of His children in this world. Each one of us has a different calling and a different function according to God's purpose. *"Now you are the body of Christ and each one of you is a part of it."* (**1 Corinthians 12:27**). In other words, we all have a unique purpose and get to participate in what God is doing in the world!

So, there are only two questions we must ask ourselves. First, when we are chosen, are we willing to respond to His call? Second, do we want to "get in the game" and be a part of what God is doing in our world today?

One of the most rewarding experiences of my life was when I was chosen by my company to be part of a team that would build a direct marketing center for our business. It was not only a promotion for me and a challenging new responsibility, but it was also an opportunity to be part of something that could be a tremendous addition to our company's business.

There were four of us selected from within the company who each had a specific skill and background for this project. My contribution to the team was in the area of customer data and analysis. One person brought sales management skills while another person brought customer messaging skills. The final person had extensive product marketing experience.

I was thrilled to be chosen to join that team. We worked well together and built a very successful operation. We received awards and recognition within our company for our work, and those work relationships turned into strong personal relationships as well. That sense of being part of something bigger than each of us was very satisfying.

God is calling each of us to be part of something bigger than ourselves. He is calling us to "leave our fishing nets behind" as Simon, Andrew, James and John did, and to follow His Son Jesus to do "even greater things" than what Jesus did. As Jesus said, *"I tell you the truth, anyone who has faith in me will do what I have been doing. He will do even greater things than these, because I am going to the Father."* (John 14:12)

Following God's call, when He chooses us, can lead to the biggest adventure of our lives. Like His first disciples, we will see miracles performed, we will see people healed from sickness, and we will see the Holy Spirit move in people's lives. We will also experience God's provision in ways we may never have seen otherwise. Answering God's call can be scary and unknown, but it will also give us blessings and the joy found in accomplishing something for Him! Jesus said, ***"Blessed rather are those who hear the word of God and obey it."*** (Luke 11:28)

In my life, God has called me by His Spirit to three different kinds of ministries. First, he called me to lead mission trips. Second, he called me into the ministry of training others, specifically church leaders and pastors. My third calling is to worship leading, using my musical gifts and love for worship.

The first call I felt from God was a call to lead mission teams. As a young child, I had always dreamed of being a bus driver. As I got older, I thought I would rather be a bus tour guide. So, when I started doing mission trips, I soon realized that I could be a mission trip leader, which is sort of like a tour guide, only for Christ instead of sightseeing. As I mentioned earlier, after I went on four mission trips, I felt the Spirit's call to take a team from our church to the mission field. I recruited the team, planned the training, and worked with an organization called Missions International who arranged all of the other logistics. Through them I led a couple of teams to Peru, and they mentored me as a trip leader as well.

As I gained knowledge and ability as a trip leader, my wife and I decided to start our own ministry so that we could lead mission teams abroad by ourselves. Our original purpose was that of training church leaders in children's, youth and adult ministries. My role was to be the mission team leader and teach on adult ministry, while Kim's was to teach about children's ministry. We added others to teach the youth ministry portion. Our early team mission trips to several nations were those kinds of trips.

I also continued to lead other teams for Missions International for a few years until our own ministry began to consume most of my time. My spiritual gifts are in the areas of administration and leadership, and so this calling was well suited to my abilities and interests. Mission trip organizing and team leading has also been the foundation for my second ministry calling, which was to the ministry of training.

I believe that God chose me to develop and teach a training course on management and leadership for pastors and church leaders in the majority world. He used a pastor in the Philippines to call me into this ministry in 2001. At the time, I was just responding to this pastor's request to help train the pastors in the region he oversaw for his church denomination. I had no idea God had something much bigger in mind!

However, I did sense the Spirit's call to help this pastor using the knowledge, gifts, education, and experience that I had to offer. It was a bit daunting and scary when I started, and there were challenges and obstacles along the way. But the Holy Spirit led me through all of them and continues to guide our training ministry to this day. By God's hand, many pastors and church leaders in the majority world have been impacted by this training. The blessings and joy I have experienced because of it have been immeasurable.

One experience I had that confirmed my calling as a trainer happened on one of our early trips to train at the Agape Bible School in Almaty, Kazakhstan. I had only been training for a few years and our training was now part of their annual curriculum. As a result, we taught a new group of students every year.

On one particular day I had the feeling that I wasn't teaching very well and not connecting with the students. I actually started to think I was unqualified to teach them, and I began to question why I was even there. This feeling grew as the day went on. I still remember thinking that I should just quit teaching altogether and that someone else more educated and knowledgeable than I should be training instead of me. I was not a pastor. What did I know about managing a church? I felt like a disreputable salesman, selling people something I knew very little about myself. By the end of the training that day, I had resolved in my mind that this would be my last trip there to train and I would stop training church leaders altogether.

At the end of our training that day, we had a question and answer session so the students could ask questions about what we taught. One of the younger female students stood up and through an interpreter said, *"I know you have doubts about why you are here training. But God has given you a gift and your teaching has been so helpful to me and the other students. God has called you here to train us and you should trust him and continue to serve him as a teacher of this material."*

I think she then asked me a question about our training, but I really don't remember. Her first comments struck me in the heart. How could she have known what I was feeling and thinking that day? Why would she start her question with that statement? But I knew that it was the Holy Spirit speaking to me. It was like getting hit upside the head with a two by four. God was trying to get my attention that I was chosen, even if I was not qualified.

I also realized that God called me for a purpose. He could have chosen anybody else to do this training, but he chose me. Why? I don't know. It doesn't matter. What matters is that He chose me, and I needed to be obedient to the Spirit's call on my life. I also recognized that it was Satan who was trying to convince me to quit and was the one filling me with doubts and insecurity. That's how Satan works. He tries to convince us that we're not worthy, qualified or acceptable to God. He is a liar! Jesus declared he is also the *"father of lies"* (**John 8:44**).

Paul wrote about being chosen in his first letter to the church at Corinth. He said, *"**Brothers, think of what you were when you were called. Not many of you were wise by human standards; not many were influential; not many were of noble birth. But God chose the foolish things of the world to shame the wise; God chose the weak things of the world to shame the strong. He chose the lowly things of this world and the despised things – and the things that are not – to nullify the things that are, so that no one can boast before him."* (**1 Corinthians 1:26-29**). This Scripture, and my experience in Kazakhstan, confirmed God's calling on my life to this ministry of training. I have never doubted that call again!

The third ministry the Spirit has called me to is worship leading. I was asked to be the worship leader for our American mission team on my very first mission trip to Kazakhstan. We had a team of 29 people and my responsibility was to lead worship for our team when we gathered for team meetings. I played the guitar and knew many worship songs, but I had never truly led worship before. I accepted the role despite my limited experience. Although I fumbled and faltered quite a bit, I eventually learned from my mistakes.

I also had the opportunity to play with the Kazakhstan worship team at our training conference, and I learned a lot from them as well. With that experience, and the encouragement of my church's worship director, I was able to grow in my ability as a worship leader. I was eventually given opportunities to lead worship in our church.

When I joined a mission team to South Africa the following year, I was asked to be the worship leader for the entire conference in both Pretoria and Durban. I had a wonderful group of musicians and singers from our team to work with, and the worship times at these conferences were very special and rewarding. I felt a great amount of joy in leading worship and being able to use my gifts of playing the guitar and singing for the Lord!

I currently play guitar in our current church's adult praise band and have had the opportunity to lead worship in our church as well. I also lead worship for our youth ministry and have led worship for children's ministry in the past. Although worship leading is not my primary ministry focus, it is a spiritual calling, and I enjoy the opportunity to lead others in worshipping the Lord whenever I am called upon to do so.

Sometimes we are chosen for something, but not necessarily called to it. One such ministry I believe I have been chosen for is preaching. While I am not a pastor, nor a Biblical scholar, I am usually asked or invited to preach when I am on a mission trip, due to my position as a ministry leader and trainer. As a guest from the USA, people from other nations often enjoy hearing a message from the Lord from visitors, especially Americans. Although I consider myself to be more of a teacher than a preacher, I do not turn down an invitation to preach, believing that the Holy Spirit is the one asking me to do so.

The first time I was invited to preach was quite an experience. It was on that same trip to South Africa where I was the worship leader in 1997. We had just arrived in the country and had only visited some of Durban that first day. Our team leader, Dr. Kent Hunter, came to me before dinner and said that he needed someone to preach at a church in Durban the next morning. All of the pastors on the team already had preaching assignments at different churches, and he thought I could preach and fill in at this one extra church that had asked for someone to come and share the Word.

Having never preached before, I was a bit hesitant. But I also knew that the Holy Spirit was asking me to step up to the challenge. So, I said yes and began to feverishly prepare to preach the next morning. I was pouring through my Bible and trying to come up with a Scripture and a message in one night. I struggled with it, but eventually put together a sermon message. I went to bed concerned that I was not prepared enough, and that my message was perhaps not as clear as I would have liked it to be. But at least I had something.

When I went down to breakfast Sunday morning, Dr. Hunter came to see me and said that I was no longer needed to preach that day. Apparently, the church had found someone else to preach instead. I was so relieved to not have to preach that morning. But it did prepare me to preach the next time God asked me to do so! And He has done that now on many occasions.

I have also had the privilege of watching God choose others or call them to ministry through His Holy Spirit as well. Let me share a few examples.

On one trip to the Philippines, I had asked a man named Greg from my church to go and help us teach at a Bible School and minister to children. Greg had previously told me that he did not have the gift of teaching children. Yet on this trip, we visited a Filipino public school where he taught and ministered to over 3,000 children! After returning to the USA, God called Him to serve in children's ministry as a teacher and he responded in faith! He would also eventually become a leader in the children's ministry at our church!

On that mission trip to South Africa in 1997, there were also several members from our church who were part of that team. One man, Kevin, was someone I knew well and admired because of his strong faith as a businessman. It was also his first international mission trip. He was part of our praise team and also did some teaching.

After that trip, I asked him to go with me on another trip to help me train pastors and church leaders. It was because I not only saw his faith in action, but I also recognized his gift of teaching. But he declined my invitation. I was a bit stunned because of our experience together in South Africa. So, I asked him why he did not want to go with me to the mission field again. He said he felt the Holy Spirit calling him to take the gospel to the business community. God had chosen him and called him to a different mission field! That was the best "no" to an invitation I have ever received!

A final example happened on a mission trip to Peru. It was the trip where I had led a team from a church in Knoxville, TN to Trujillo in 2007. One of the team members, a man named Les, was on his first international mission trip. On this trip he had the opportunity to let the Holy Spirit use him in several different ways.

He did church construction work, some children's ministry, and also participated in some evangelism calls. He was so moved by his experiences in Peru that when he returned to the USA, he started his own mission ministry to Peru! He returned there annually and began working in a poor community that needed help. He even recruited others to go with him!

What a joy and a blessing it is to witness God choosing others to go and minister where He sends them, and to see them respond to the Holy Spirit's calling on their lives!

I would encourage you to think back on your life and the times that you were chosen for something. Perhaps it was for a sports team, a job, a school, or an award of some kind. How did that make you feel? Were you grateful, proud, or excited? Did you feel lucky or fortunate? Or did you sense God's presence in the process of being chosen?

God is always involved in our being chosen for something because He desires to see His will brought about through each of us. He will direct others to see us as He sees us and to do what is needed according to His will. He will already have prepared us for being chosen as well, if we are the person He has called. No one chooses the purpose for which God calls them. Instead, God reveals His purpose for us through His calling.

And when we are not chosen, we must accept that decision as well and trust that it was not meant for us. We need to know and understand that God had a different purpose and plan in mind for our lives. So, we must continue to pray for His will for our life and seek His calling along a different path.

Being chosen by God and called by His Spirit is a privilege and an honor. It is the most rewarding experience that I have had in my lifetime. It's such a blessing to know that God chooses us for His purposes. His Spirit prepares us, provides for us, and goes with us to lead and guide us to accomplish His will. We are never left on the sidelines unless we choose not to participate by rejecting His call. We are never considered worthless or unusable.

The Bible tells us about one person who was considered useless. It was a slave named Onesimus. He ran away from his owner, Philemon, and met up with Paul while he was in prison. He became a dear son in the Lord to Paul. But Paul sent him back to Philemon, and wrote to Philemon that he should welcome him because *"Formerly he was useless to you, but now he has become useful both to you and to me."* (**Philemon 11**).

God wants to use all of His children. None of us are useless. We are gifted by God and then chosen and called by His Spirit to serve Him and others in Jesus name. Let us not close our ears or heart to His call, but eagerly respond yes, and experience the blessing of being chosen!

Chapter 7

LESSON #5: GOD PROVIDES FOR US

*"Command those who are rich in this world not to be
arrogant nor to put their hope in wealth, which is so
uncertain, but to put their hope in God, who richly
provides us with everything for our enjoyment."*
1 Timothy 6:17

The Scriptures talk about God's provision for His
people, but also the entire human race. God created the earth and all that is in it, including food, shelter
and clothing. From the moment He created man, He
has provided for all humans. The fact that some people
have very little and some people have more is not a
result of God's lack or abundance of provision. It is
because of man's greed and selfishness.

When I was in college and studying international
economics, I remember asking my professor why
the excess food America produced wasn't given to
starving people in Africa. He said that it was, but that
sending them our excess food was not the problem. The
problem was that governments in other nations often

don't distribute the food fairly, or the food is confis-
cated by others.

You might remember that in the early 1990's the
United States sent food to the starving people of Somalia.
But local warlords were confiscating the food supplies.
So, the United States sent Army Rangers into Somalia
to make sure the food we sent them got to the starving
people. That situation was the basis for the movie *Black
Hawk Down*. In other words, the issue wasn't the avail-
ability of food for those starving, but rather making sure
it got to the people who really needed it.

When God created the earth, He made plants and
animals that would be designed for our consumption,
our clothing and our shelter. He built them into his creation so that we humans would have a regenerating
supply of these things to sustain us in this world. It's
pretty amazing when we stop to think about it. God's
design of the earth provided the basics of life that we
need to live, including sunlight, oxygen, water, food,
proteins, vitamins, heating materials, and building
materials.

God also gave us brains and the intelligence to learn
how to use these life resources, and to develop them to
where they are today. And I believe that we will continue to develop them further to meet the needs of a
growing population on the earth according to God's
purpose and will.

There's a story I heard about an argument between
Satan and God. Satan was telling God that he could
make everything that God has made. He even boasted
that he could make man. God said that he couldn't. But
Satan said, "I can prove it to you." So, he bent down and
started to pick up some dirt. God said, "Wait a minute,
you make your own dirt!"

People who believe in science and the big bang theory can never quite explain how anything came into existence. They claim it all just happened. But if it all just happened, how was everything designed to work in the way it does? They can never answer that question because, at some point, they have to acknowledge some sort of creator. Since they don't believe that God was the Creator, they have no one or nothing else to point to as the designer of our universe.

Our world, and the earth itself, lead to the conclusion that there is an intelligent design. And that only leaves God as the one who designed it all for us. The earth has no other purpose than to be a home for mankind. That's why it was created in the first place. Fortunately, God also provided everything we need to not only sustain life, but to enjoy it as well!

Anyone living today did absolutely nothing to be here on the earth. They were created by God in their mother's womb. *"For you created my inmost being; you knit me together in my mother's womb."* (**Psalm 139:13**). And since their birth, they initially relied on their parents to provide for them physically until they could provide for themselves as an adult. But no human being has ever created anything original. They have only created things from what the Creator has already provided! We just simply learn more about them and put them together in ways that makes something else.

It was also God's design that we have the creativity and intelligence to do that. Once we acknowledge that God created everything, we then must acknowledge that He provided the materials that we need and the ability to learn how to use them as well!

I have been blessed to travel the world and visit many countries and cultures. I have experienced

79

God's wonderful creation being used and put together in so many different ways. From the rice terraces in the Philippines, to the pyramids of Egypt, to the city of Machu Picchu in the Andes mountains, to the silk clothing in India, to the aqueducts of Rome, to the spices of the Caribbean, to the wood carvings of Africa, to the Great Wall of China, and to the stunning architectural buildings of Singapore, what man has made or produced from what God has provided is truly astounding. But what is most important is that God provided all of the basics that we needed first, along with the creativity and intelligence on how to use them.

In order to go and train pastors around the world, I must rely on God's provision to do His work. I raise the funds needed to pay for our travel, the training by our global trainers, and our family income. These are all necessary to do what we do. And God has never failed to provide for us and our ministry. However, on some of my various trips, I have needed God's extra provision above and beyond our ministry and family needs. Consequently, I have experienced several situations when God provided for me or others in only a way that He can.

The first occurrence I witnessed of God's amazing provision was in Kazakhstan in October of 1996. It was my second international mission trip, but the first for my wife, Kim. Both of us were invited to join a worship ministry team from Charlotte, NC. I taught a workshop on Christian music as an evangelistic tool and Kim was invited to teach workshops on drama for worship and children's music. Her first workshop on drama came up the first day after our morning plenary session. We gathered in a nearby school in a small classroom that held about 30 people, similar to an American public school.

Kim had an interpreter assigned to her for this session so that her teaching in English would be translated into Russian for the attendees.

Before the session started, she met her interpreter, Victor, and went over the training material with him while 70 attendees squeezed into the classroom for the upcoming session. It was a packed house! When it was time to start, she began to speak by introducing herself, and Victor began to translate. He seemed a bit nervous and was struggling with a few words, but that is often normal at the beginning of a session when a translator is hearing the speaker for the first time. However, Victor continued to struggle and after about 15 minutes excused himself to go use the bathroom.

So, we all sat there and waited for him to return, which he did in a couple of minutes. Kim resumed teaching and within a few minutes, Victor excused himself again rather abruptly and left the room. We thought that he might have some stomach problems, so we waited for him to return once again. But after waiting about five minutes he still wasn't back. So, I went to the bathroom to see if he was okay. But when I got there, he said to me that he was so ill he could not go on.

I went back to the classroom and told Kim that Victor was not coming back. As you can probably imagine, without a translator she could not teach at all. I could see the look of disappointment on her face. She had come all this way to teach her workshop and she had no interpreter to translate for her. We discussed our options, and I suggested that I could go and find our team leaders to see if there was another translator available. However, they were all scattered in different classrooms, and as far as I knew, all of the other translators were in use.

So, out of desperation, Kim turned and addressed the classroom and simply asked if anyone there spoke English and could translate for her, not thinking anyone could. There was a man in the back of the room who raised his hand and said that he spoke a little English. She asked him if he would be willing to translate for her as we had no other option. He said he was not that fluent, but he would try. His name was Marat. Marat came forward and immediately began to translate for Kim and did very well. We were all surprised as he seemed to be a better translator than Victor, the original interpreter who had been assigned to Kim.

We later learned that it was the first time that Victor had translated in public. He was so nervous that he became sick to his stomach and literally could not do the translating. But Marat was able to step in for him when it was needed. Marat had no idea he would be needed to translate that day. Yet God provided him for Kim when we all thought there wasn't a translator available.

Another experience of God's provision in a crisis happened to me in India during the Iceland volcanic eruption in 2010. Because of that, there was volcanic ash in the air that had grounded all flights through the northern part of Europe. I had already been in India for four days when the eruption occurred and the ash started affecting flights. By the time I returned to Mumbai to take my flight home to the USA, there had already been 10 days of cancelations of all flights going through northern Europe.

When I got to my hotel near the airport in Mumbai for my flight home, I checked the flight status in the hope that my flight that night would be the first one they let leave. If not, I could be stuck in India for at least ten days since there were ten days of flight cancelations ahead of me with travelers also wanting to get back home.

When I first checked the status in the middle of the afternoon, my Delta/KLM flight was still showing an on-time departure to Amsterdam. I remember praying that it would be allowed to take off that night. Since it had not been canceled yet, perhaps there was still a chance. But about an hour later, I checked back and the flight had been canceled. So, I called my travel agent in the USA who had made the reservations in hope that she could get me on another flight. But she said she couldn't. She said since Delta canceled the flight, I had to go to the airport and talk directly with Delta there to make other arrangements.

By that time it was around 6 pm and I knew there was nothing then I could do to resolve the problem. So, I went out to dinner to consider my next steps and the potential options I could discuss with Delta.

At around 9 pm I took a taxi to the airport, which was only 15 minutes away from my hotel, and went to the Delta check-in counter. I told the agent my situation and asked about my options. He said *"just a minute,"* and typed something into his computer and stared at it for a little bit. Then he looked down near my feet and asked me if I had my luggage with me. I said no because I had not planned on leaving tonight since the flight was canceled. He looked at me and said, *"How fast can you get back here with your luggage? I may be able to get you on another flight leaving in a few hours."* I said I was at a hotel 15 minutes away and could be back in 40 minutes with my luggage. He said if you can get back here quickly, I think I can put you on this other flight.

I dashed out of the terminal and got a taxi back to my hotel. However, the taxi driver did not recognize my hotel name and did not know where it was. I thought to myself, this was the last thing I needed. I have an opportunity to go home tonight and not spend another 10 days in India and I get a taxi driver that does not know the area around the airport or my hotel. How is that possible? I prayed in the taxi while he drove around the area searching for my hotel. I asked the Holy Spirit to help the taxi driver and me to find my hotel.

When I finished praying, I looked up and I saw a local train station on the right side of the street. I remembered that our hotel was across the street from a train station. I immediately looked over to the left side and saw our hotel and told the driver where it was. He pulled in and I told him not to move. I said I was getting my luggage and would be back down in five minutes and to wait for me. I did not want to waste time trying to hail another taxi back to the airport.

I quickly went up to my room, got my luggage, and then checked out as quickly as possible. We were on our way back to the airport in about 10 minutes. When we got to the airport, I paid the driver and rushed in with my bags and went straight to the Delta ticket agent. He was able to get me the last available seat on a Jet Airways flight to Newark! That flight was allowed to leave because it was flying through Athens, Greece, which is in the southern part of Europe and not affected by the volcanic ash like Amsterdam.

I was so grateful for the ticket and rushed off to go through security and passport control and get to the gate to board the flight. But then I began to wonder about my seat assignment. I figured it would be in the middle seat in the last row of the airplane, which would have been uncomfortable at best on such a long flight. But at that point I just thanked God for the flight that night, and was grateful to be heading home and not having to spend ten more days in India!

When I finally looked at my boarding pass, I realized that I had the middle seat in the very first row of economy, often referred to as the bulkhead. When I boarded the plane, I quickly saw that there was extra legroom in that row and plenty of space to get around the person on the aisle. Although it was a middle seat, it was a very comfortable seat for the 20 hour journey to Newark. So, not only did God provide me a ticket home, but He also gave me a comfortable seat as well!

God also provided a flight home for me and my training partner in 2014 after the original flight we were booked on was canceled.

We were on our way back from Nepal and had a stopover in Bangkok for a day to do some sightseeing. We took an all day tour to go see the Bridge on the River Kwai (of WWII history and movie fame), as well as a floating market and Tiger habitat. When we arrived back at our hotel in Bangkok after the tour, we both got messages from Delta that our flight the next morning from Bangkok to Tokyo had been canceled. Since we could not make our connecting flight to Atlanta in Tokyo they had put us on the same flights a day later.

However, my training partner had to be back for an important meeting the day after our original arrival and he wanted to look for other options that would get us home the next day as planned. So, he called Delta and they said they could route us through Beijing and Seattle and get us back home to Atlanta at about the same time as our original flight. The only issue was that the flight from Bangkok to Beijing left in a few hours and we needed to get to the airport right away to make that flight. We quickly packed our bags, checked out of our hotel, headed to the airport, and made the flight that night to Beijing. It was not a Delta flight but on a Chinese airline that was very nice as well as on-time!

When we arrived in Beijing, we had a fairly short layover. But the bigger problem was that we had no visa to go through China, which neither of us had thought about. As we went through immigration in Beijing, we told them our story and said we had no transit visa. The immigration officer said that was okay, but that we would likely not make our flight to Seattle. But she allowed us through anyway to try.

Since we were connecting from a Chinese airline, we had to go to the Delta check-in counter to check our bags and get our boarding passes. The ticket counter was almost closed, but they saw us running and quickly took our bags and checked us in. Next, we had to go through security to get to the flight and there was only about 30 minutes left before departure. As expected, there was a line. Fortunately, we got through the line in 15 minutes and dashed off to catch the plane.

My travel partner wanted a cup of coffee so he stopped to buy one in the terminal as I rushed to get on the plane and let them know he was still coming. When he finally got on the plane a few minutes after me, he did not have a cup of coffee with him. I asked him if there was a problem getting coffee and he said no. He said that when he got to the gate, he was not allowed to take it on the plane according to Chinese regulations. So, he had to dump it all! We laughed about that but were also grateful to be on our way home.

So, God provided a flight home that met our needs. On top of that, He also put in business class from Seattle back to Atlanta! Our God is an awesome God!

I had a different kind of transportation experience in Pretoria, South Africa that demonstrated God's provision, although it was actually somewhat humorous. We were taking a bus from Johannesburg to Pretoria (about a one hour drive) to begin a conference on Church Growth there. As we headed on our way, our team learned that the bus driver that was hired was not familiar with the church in Pretoria we were teaching at and did not know where it was. This was in 1997 and well before the days of cell phones and GPS, especially in South Africa. Our team leader decided that when we got to Pretoria we would ask someone for directions.

When we arrived in Pretoria, we pulled over near someone walking along the street and asked him where the church was. He gave us directions and our bus driver proceeded to follow them, but we never found the church. It was apparent that the directions were missing something, or we took a wrong turn somewhere. So, the bus driver pulled over again and we asked someone else on the street where the church was. They also gave us directions, which were different from the first person, and off we went to find the church. Again, we could not find it and saw nothing that led us to believe we were even close to it. Our team leaders began to get nervous now because we needed to be there early to setup and prepare for the conference, and we were already going to be late as it was.

So, our team leader told our bus driver to pull over near a convenience store. He got out and went in to ask someone about the church and maybe see a local city map. There was a man in the store who overheard our leader ask about the church and he said he knew the church and where it was. He also offered to lead us there in his car. Not wanting to be late, our leader said okay. The man got into his car and we followed him in the bus. And he took us right to the church!

The funny part was that the church was what we, in America, call a mega church. It was huge and seated perhaps ten thousand people. It also sat high upon a hill so that it could be seen for miles around! I am sure we must have passed by it several times and never realized it was the church we were looking for. In our time of distress and crisis, God provided a person to show us the way! God provided a man to help us that day, just as He also provided His own Son Jesus to show us the way to Him!

I have also experienced God's provision of finances on the first trip I led to Cape Town, South Africa in 2002. Our host wanted a large amount of money to cover his expenses for advertising and recruiting people to attend our training. It was way more than I antici-pated and budgeted for. But I had already committed to the trip and had recruited our team members, so I felt that I could not back out now. I was able to nego-tiate a reduction in what we would provide to him, but I was still concerned about having enough money in our budget to cover the cost of everything we would need in South Africa. But I put my trust in the Lord and believed that He would work it all out and provide what was needed.

Well, as it turned out, the Rand (South African currency) was very cheap against the US dollar that year. We also went in June, which is their wintertime, and the hotels and other costs were much lower than anticipated. Furthermore, we discovered that the food costs were much lower than what I had estimated, due to the lower currency value. I could literally take our entire team of 12 people and our hosts out to dinner at a very nice restaurant and still only spend roughly $5 US per person!

At the end of the trip the money we saved on hotel, food and other costs offset the amount we paid to our host for his advertising and recruiting expenses. Consequently, our total costs came in right at what we budgeted. God provided exactly what was needed!

So, whether it was transportation, people or finances, God has always provided! I have come to learn this first hand and see how He meets our needs when we are called according to His purpose! God confirmed what Hudson Taylor, a missionary to China, had once said, *"God's work done in God's way never lacks God's supply!"*

But God's provision is not just meant for those who serve in ministry positions. He extends His provision to all of His children. Have you thought about God's provision in your life? If you have a home, a job, a car, or a wife & children, do you realize that these have come from God as well? These are all things that He alone provides and for which you and I should recognize and be grateful for. God also provides strength in times of weakness, courage in times of fear, and wisdom in times of indecision. He also provides healing, comfort and mercy in abundance.

I would encourage you to think about all of the ways that God has provided for you. Do not limit your thinking to just the physical things, but consider the spiritual things as well. When you do that, you will see that God has provided for you abundantly. And God will show you that everything you have comes from Him (**James 1:17**).

Chapter 8

LESSON #6: GOD WORKS THROUGH US

*"For it is God who works in you to will
and to act in order to fulfill His good purpose."*
Philippians 2:13

One of the concerns that many people have is to be used or manipulated by others. I don't know if this comes from our sense of free will and the liberty to make our own choices in life, but it seems to be a common attitude among Americans. This concern is what also often breeds skepticism and caution in our relationships with others, particularly people we do not know well. Perhaps it is simply an acknowledgement that there are people out there who would take advantage of our gullibility to give them money or information that could be used to drain our bank accounts. But we know they do exist and are thus warned to be aware of scams, whether on the telephone, the internet or in person. While we might have a great compassion to help people, we must also be discerning as to what is real and what is not. Otherwise, we could be easily misled, and it could cost us our money, trust or security.

In general, I think most people are trusting of others, but cautious. If we know someone well, then we have more trust in them. But if we don't, we often look for warning signs that a person is who they say they are or purport to be, or if something they tell us does not sound right or seems a bit off. These warning signs can save us from making a poor decision or, at a minimum, give us more time to look for further information to determine their credibility. The point is that we don't want others to use us for their purposes, or manipulate us into doing or buying something that benefits them and not us.

I would imagine that most of us have been used or manipulated at some time in our life. It has happened to me on a few occasions. I've been used by a former boss to help them advance their career. I've been manipulated by someone I love to do something I later regretted. I am now skeptical of strangers who approach me and want to shake my hand. It's because I once had a salesman do that who would not let go until he made his sales pitch to me. I am also cautious about emails I receive asking for financial help or offering access to available funds. I'm sure you could share your own stories with me as well. So, we are all a bit more hesitant today to take everything at face value, sometimes even from people we know and trust. We just do not like to be used or manipulated by other people.

We often respond in the same way when we are asked to submit to others, usually bosses, coaches, ministry leaders or community officials. We tend to be cautious if we don't really know them well or are not sure of their motivation.

The Bible talks about submission quite a bit. We are told to *"submit to God"* (James 4:7), to *"submit to one another"* (**Ephesians 5:21**), to *"submit to the author-ities"* (**Romans 13:1**), to *"submit to our masters"* (**1 Peter 2:18**), and to *"submit to our leaders"* (**Hebrews 13:17**). But being the self-centered and sinful people we are, we don't like to submit to others. We want to do what we want to do. We want to make our own decisions and rely on our own judgment. The only time we generally submit to someone else is when we believe they know more than we do, and so we trust their judgment instead of ours.

In America, and many nations around the world today, we are placing our trust in scientists and government leaders to handle our current corona virus global pandemic. We are submitting to their leadership and recommendations because we don't have the experience or information they have to make our own judgment on what to do. But I can only imagine the anger that might result if at some point in the future we learn that we were misled or manipulated for political or economic reasons. If that happens, we will be less likely to submit to them ever again.

As Christians and followers of Christ, we are called to submit our lives to God. Why? It is because He loves us and wants the best for us. God is Good. God is Holy. God is Love. God is Truth. God is Light. There is nothing false in Him. God wants to bless us and give us hope and joy in our lives today. He waits patiently for us to call upon Him so He can give us His best. He promises that if we give to Him and others, He will give even more back to us. Jesus said, *"Give and it will be given to you. A good measure, pressed down, shaken together and running over, will be poured into your lap. For with the measure you use, it will be measured to you."*(**Luke 6:38**)

But submission comes at a cost. It is the cost of our own will. We must be willing to trust in God enough to turn over control of our lives to Him so that He can use us to do His will in our lives. You see, God indeed wants to **_use_** us for His purposes. He wants to work through us to accomplish His will for others and for His creation. But for Him to do so, we must submit ourselves to Him. Unfortunately, so often we find it difficult as humans to do that. Perhaps we're afraid of losing control of our lives. Or maybe we don't want to be changed and would rather hold on to our earthly desires or possessions. Whatever the reason, many Christians find it hard to submit to God in **_all_** things.

I would have to admit that I don't submit my life to God in all things. I know that is not what He wants or what is best for me. But I believe it's because of my sinful nature and desire to do what I want rather than what He might want at times. I have confessed this sin to God, and He continues to forgive me and show me that His way is better.

I do believe that when it comes to our global training ministry, however, I more readily submit to God and pray for His will to be done through me when I travel, train and minister in Jesus' name! It is because it is **_His_** ministry. And He has shown me how He has worked through me and others when we submit to His will and purpose. Let me now share a few examples from some of our mission trips of how God has used me and others to accomplish His will.

Perhaps the first such realization I had about God using me was on a trip I led to Cape Town, South Africa in 2002. This trip was organized to provide children, youth and adult ministry training in three cities around Cape Town. I had recruited a team of about 12 people to come and train for three days in each location. We also visited some local ministries and churches while we were there, which is always a joy. Our local host had arranged for us to split up into groups and visit several churches one Sunday, and I was asked to preach at one of the churches, which I gladly accepted. By this time, I was prepared to preach!

That day was somewhat cool, and I decided to wear a red sweater over my shirt and tie instead of my sport jacket. It was unusual for me to do that, but I reasoned that it might be cold in the church or easier to shed my sweater later in the day. As I preached that morning, I felt as though I was not connecting with the people. When I train people or speak to groups, I try to read my audience so that I can see if I am connecting or making sense. I felt as though my message that day was weak and that I had not done a very good job. My strength is teaching, not preaching, so I finished up and hoped that I was misreading the congregation and that my message was actually fine.

It was the custom of this church for the preacher to go to the front door after the service to greet the people as they left. As the people filed out of the church, I had lots of smiles and handshakes but no comments about my sermon. I began to think that I was right about my weak message and poor performance in the pulpit. Towards the end of the line a woman came through, shook my hand, and said that she thought my message was meant specifically for her, and that she deeply appreciated my sermon.

I was shocked a bit since she was the only one to comment on my message that morning. She went on to tell me that during the previous night the Holy Spirit came to her in her sleep and told her that He would send a man in a **_red sweater_** to speak a message to her! And she told me that the message I brought that day was exactly what she needed to hear! I was amazed that God would use me to speak a word to one person out of a congregation of over a hundred people! But that's what I believe He did. And I know that both the woman and I were blessed that day, even if no one else was!

A somewhat similar experience happened to me on one of my early trips to India where we held a training conference in the city of Bangalore. We had about 60 attendees and the training seemed to go very well based on the participation and engagement of the participants in our questions and exercises. The Indian culture is male dominated and so it was not unusual that the women rarely spoke up or asked questions. Fortunately, we were able to teach in English and so we could talk to the participants during breaks and before and after our sessions.

On one of the last days of training, I was talking to a group of young women during a tea break. I decided to ask them what they thought of the training to get their feedback. One of them, Sumitra, said that she decided to come to the training at the very last minute. She had been very frustrated in her ministry and had planned to quit. She only came to the training because she had committed to do so and felt obligated to show up. When I asked her why she wanted to quit, she said that she wasn't connecting with the people in her ministry group and thought that she was not cut out for ministry work.

So, I asked her what she thought of our training. She said that it completely changed her attitude. She said our training was showing her that she had been making some mistakes and that it gave her some practical tools and ideas of how to minister more effectively.

She went on to say that she would not quit her ministry, but instead would go back and use our training to adjust her approach. She now felt more confident about serving the Lord in her calling because of what she learned by attending our training conference.

Her testimony helped me realize that the Holy Spirit was using us to reach others for His purposes in their lives. It was a great reminder that God will use anyone to reach anyone that He has called to serve Him. Although I am not sure today what happened to Sumitra and her ministry (since I have not been back to Bangalore since then), I am confident that at least at that moment God's Spirit put us in her pathway and used us to encourage her to continue her ministry. God had not given up on Sumitra. And who knows how many others have been blessed and encouraged by her!

Whenever I go and train, I am primarily training pastors and church leaders. But there have been occasions where there have been others attending our training. One of the more interesting experiences I had took place in Nicaragua in 2011.

We were training at a local missionary school, but the conference was also open to pastors and church leaders from the local community. One couple from the community, a husband and wife, sat in the front row. Throughout the training they were both very engaged in it, asking many questions and participating fully in all of the exercises. They were also highly educated and appeared very professional and knowledgeable.

On the second day of training I asked our hosts who they were, as others seemed to know them and showed respect to them. Our host said that the wife was the Court Judge of the local community and her husband was a prominent lawyer in the community. He also told me that the wife was a committed Christian, but her husband was not a Believer. I was literally shocked that such a highly educated man and a non-Christian would attend one of our training conferences. Our training is very basic and Biblically based, so I never considered that someone like him would ever want to attend. But I'm also confident that his wife had some influence in his being there! We had the opportunity to meet them both and talk with them through an interpreter, and it was wonderful to have them attend our training.

But what surprised me the most was that, after the conference concluded and we had handed out certificates to everyone, including this couple, I saw a group of pastors praying over the Judge's husband in the back of the room. As I watched, I was wondering what they were praying over him about. When I asked my host what he knew, he told me this lawyer had accepted the Lord and was becoming a Believer in Christ! I was totally amazed! Through all the training I had ever conducted up until that time I had never given thought that a non-Believer would attend our training, let alone accept Christ as well.

I do not think that it was our training alone that caused his conversion, but it was certainly part of the process that the Holy Spirit was using to draw this man to Him. I honestly believe that the spiritual environment of the training had the greatest impact, because not only was he receiving God's Word, he was interacting with other Christian pastors and leaders from his community, and that seemed to greatly affect him. It was a joy to be used by God and to watch His Holy Spirit complete the work He began in this lawyer's life! As the Bible says, ***"He who began a good work in you will***

carry it on to completion until the day of Jesus Christ."
(Philippians 1:6)

God has also used me to encourage many others in their walk of faith, especially those I have taken with me to the mission field. I have seen mission team members get more involved in their churches and ministries after a mission trip experience that I led. I saw one young woman change her college major as a result of her experience on one of our mission trips. I saw another woman come back from a mission trip experience to become deeply involved in another ministry. I also witnessed a church recognize the mission field of the poor in their own community after ministering to the poor in another country.

I have also invited friends from our church with a business background and the gift of teaching to go and train with me, knowing that it would give them a different perspective on the world and increase their faith. And it always did! Some of them continue to go and train with me to this day. Others have gone on mission trips with other organizations to serve in ways that they are most gifted. It is always a blessing to see how God uses us to strengthen the faith of others and lead them into their own ministry.

There are also many of our global trainers who have shared their testimonies with me about our training and its impact on them, their churches, and their ministries. I often share them in our ministry newsletters and website blogs so that our supporters and others can see how our ministry is impacting the lives of pastors and church leaders around the world.

God is at the center of our ministry and uses us to accomplish His purposes in others. It is such a tremendous blessing to see the Holy Spirit work through us and to watch Him change lives. This is not unusual at all, but rather the typical experience that we have serving Him. God not only calls us to ministry, but His Holy Spirit also works through us to bring about His will for others! It is a blessing just to be a part of His Plan!

God wants to use you as well to accomplish His purposes. If I were to ask you how God has worked through you to impact others in your life, what would you say? Have you introduced Jesus to anyone and seen them come to faith? Have you experienced answered prayer when praying for a friend? Have others mentioned your role in their faith journey as part of their testimony? Have you ever felt God saying to you, *"well done, good and faithful servant!"*? If you have, God has used you to impact the life of another! And He has also revealed that to you.

But if you are not sure, perhaps God has not finished His work just yet. I would encourage you to step out in faith and follow the Lord's prompting to invite someone to your home, your church, your Bible study group, or a Christian concert/movie. Maybe there is someone that you can help or serve in some way. These are all opportunities to share your faith with others and let God use you to lead them to Him.

In order to have God work through us we must submit ourselves to His will. God will use us, and work through us, if we let Him.

Chapter 9

LESSON# 7: GOD SPEAKS FOR US

"Moses said to the Lord, 'Oh Lord, I have never been eloquent, neither in the past nor since you have spoken to your servant. I am slow of speech and tongue'. The Lord said to him, 'Who gave man his mouth? Who makes him deaf or mute? Who gives him sight or makes him blind? Is it not I, the Lord? Now go; I will help you speak and will teach you what to say.'"
Exodus 4:10-12

As a general rule, I am not a quiet person. Of course, there are times I choose to be silent. But if I have something to say, most of the time I usually say it, whether in a meeting, in a classroom, on a telephone call, or in a personal conversation. I enjoy conversation and like to spend time talking to others and I rarely run out of things to say. Sometimes I feel as though I talk too much, and so I need to be aware of that and be careful not to dominate a conversation.

I am also uncomfortable with silence when the situation calls for someone to speak, such as in a class when the instructor asks a question. If no one else answers, I feel a compulsion to say something to fill in the silence.

I have also been a public speaker for many years. It started when I was working in my business career and had opportunities to give presentations at business luncheons, corporate meetings, and national conferences. I am used to speaking in public and being in front of people. For many people, that is their greatest fear. But I have always enjoyed it as long as I was prepared and felt I had something valuable to say or speak about.

For the past 20 years, I have been training pastors and church leaders around the world on our Management for Church Leaders™ training, and I truly enjoy teaching others. Of course, it's easier when you know the material well and have been teaching it for a long time. But when I started teaching, I wasn't as effective a teacher as I am today. As my pastor often says, practice makes progress!

The Lord has given me the spiritual gift of teaching and that has helped me a lot. And I've gotten much better over the years in my abilities because I use it all the time. Because it is a gift from the Lord, it is never difficult or a burden to me. In general, I can speak clearly and coherently, even when under pressure or when I have to think on my feet, such as in a television or radio interview.

God has also given me the gift of words and writing. I have gained a lot of experience writing from my college education in economics, which always required written papers and presentations. I also was taught how to write executive briefings, reports and proposals in my business career. I have also been a songwriter for many years and have shared my music in churches and other venues. These have all served to give me a great deal of experience in writing and public speaking.

What this all implies is that I am seldom at a loss for words. Whether I am teaching, preaching, being interviewed or making presentations, I am generally well prepared to handle those opportunities without fear or anxiety. I am comfortable speaking in front of people and knowing what needs to be said, or how I can contribute to a discussion or conversation. So, I usually don't have a problem coming up with the words I should say in a particular situation, though I will admit I have put my foot in my mouth a few times!

There is one well-known example from the Bible of a person who had issues with public speaking. His name was Moses. He even begged the Lord not to have to go and speak to Pharaoh as God had instructed him. Moses said to God, *"Oh Lord, I have never been eloquent, neither in the past nor since you have spoken to your servant. I am slow of speech and tongue."* (**Exodus 4:10**) God responded to Moses by telling him, *"Now go; I will help you and teach you what to say."* (**Exodus 4:12**)

Like Moses, there are times that we ourselves lack the words to say, or we fall silent when asked to either proclaim or defend our faith. The Apostle Paul said, *"In the same way, the Spirit helps us in our weakness. We do not know what we ought to pray for, but the Spirit himself intercedes for us through wordless groans."* (**Romans 8:26**) God was declaring that even if we don't know what to say, His Holy Spirit will give us the words, just as He did for Moses.

There were several times that I recall the Lord speaking for me as well, giving me the words to say when I wasn't sure what to say or how to say it. Let me share a few examples.

After teaching our Management for Church Leaders training over several years to many pastors, church leaders and Bible students in the Philippines, I decided it would be worthwhile to visit some of them and see how our training had impacted their ministries. So, in August of 2007, our primary contact in the Philippines had arranged for me to visit 21 churches in the northern part of the island of Luzon where we had trained their pastors. He had arranged visits to seven of them a day for three days. Most of those visits consisted of conversations over coffee or tea and snacks with the pastors at the churches during the day. All of those discussions were very helpful and gave us good insight into the application of our teaching and its impact.

However, on the last day when we arrived at the 21st and final church, there was a large group gathered in a tent. We were brought inside and they were in the midst of a worship service. I thought this was quite fitting for our final church visit until the pastor came over to me and told me I was preaching in five minutes! I was immediately taken aback and was not prepared to preach. At that time in our ministry, I had preached on occasion but had always been asked ahead of time so that I had time to prepare a sermon. But on this day, I was thrust into having to think quickly and come up with something to preach on.

So, the first thing that came to my mind was to pray and ask the Holy Spirit to give me a Scripture to pray from. He guided me towards **Jeremiah 29:11**, which was one of my favorite Bible verses that says, *"For I know the plans I have for you, declares the Lord, plans to prosper you and not to harm you, plans to* *give you hope and a future."* But I did not feel I was to preach on that verse that day. He next led me to **Jeremiah 29:13**, just two verses later. This Scripture says, *"You will seek me and find me when you seek me with all your heart."* The Holy Spirit confirmed that verse to me and I began to think about what I could say.

All of a sudden I was introduced and called up to preach the message. I literally had almost no idea of what I was going to say as I was walking up to the lectern. I just prayed that the Holy Spirit would speak through me somehow.

I began by reading the Scripture verse and said a few words about what that seemed to be saying. While I was doing that, the Holy Spirit reminded me of a story about our daughter playing a game of "hide and seek" at our church about 15 years earlier. It literally came out of nowhere, and so I knew that the Holy Spirit had brought it to my mind. I used that story as an illustration of how God never plays "hide and seek" with us. The goal of the game is to hide and not let anyone find you. The last person found is the winner. But God never hides and always wants us to find Him. He's actually the worst "hide and seek" player of all time because He doesn't hide and wants to be found first!

The Holy Spirit then led me to other connected stories and Scriptures and before I knew it, I had preached an entire sermon! That was a wonderful lesson to learn about how the Holy Spirit spoke through me, even when I did not know what I was going to say! I have also heard testimonies from others I have taken to the mission field that had that same experience!

When we train in other nations, we arrange to have interpreters who translate what we teach in English into the local language so it can be understood. It is very rare that I get the opportunity to train solely in English. The only language I can speak reasonably well, other than English, is Spanish. I took four years of Spanish in school and had a good working knowledge of it. But I was not fluent. I had grown in my Spanish speaking ability but was not at a point where I felt I could comfortably teach in Spanish. I thought it was always best to use an interpreter so that the attendees got a better speaker of the language, and also someone who could put our training into their cultural and church context.

On one occasion in Peru I was teaching a session on children's ministry. It was not my teaching, but actually a teaching that my wife had developed. I was merely reading and teaching what she had written. The translator, who the local church had arranged for my session, was having a great deal of difficulty interpreting for me that day. It could have been nervousness or lack of experience translating in a church environment. I'm not sure which. But it was very difficult for her and she was struggling with each sentence. I continually had to give her the Spanish words for what I was teaching. Eventually it got to the point where it was just easier for me to teach in Spanish myself, which is what I ended up doing.

My teaching ended up being basic and simple, but seemed to be effective. Consequently, the Holy Spirit was able to help me teach in Spanish, a language I knew but was not proficient in. God can step in and take over and speak for us, even in another language, when necessary!

There are also times when the Holy Spirit urges us to say something that we might not feel comfortable saying. I was once preaching to a large congregation in Almaty, Kazakhstan where I had preached several times before. The people there knew me well and I felt comfortable sharing the Word with them.

This particular time I had chosen to give a message on the two sides of confession. One side is that we confess our sins and the second side is that we confess our faith. I had actually written a song on that subject. It was not only the basis for my sermon, but I had planned to sing it for them that morning as well. Having been there many times, I was always a little disappointed that they, like many Pentecostal churches, did not have any type of corporate confession of sin or use any of the Christian creeds in their services.

So, at the urging of the Holy Spirit, I decided that I would incorporate the confessions we use in our Lutheran church service into my sermon message that morning. I actually took the confession of sins that we use in our church liturgy word for word, and also the Apostle's Creed, and had them repeat them with me (in Russian) during my sermon message. But I did not tell them where they came from or that they were from our Lutheran service. I was a little bit apprehensive about that and was worried I might have overstepped my bounds.

But after the church service quite a few people came up to me and through my interpreter told me how much they enjoyed the message, especially the confession of sins and the confession of faith. I was relieved that they found them inspiring and beneficial, and felt blessed that I had listened to the Lord's prompting and used them!

A similar situation also happened in Lagos, Nigeria, but in the opposite way. Normally when I teach our training, I use examples from the Bible or my church experience to illustrate key points and principles. I try very hard not to mention anything political or negative about other churches or pastors. But on this occasion, when I was teaching about Making Disciples, I mentioned an American pastor who I thought was leading his followers away from God and the Scriptures. I talked about his lavish lifestyle, his crafting of his public image, and his reticence to speak the whole truth of the Bible, especially about sin and repentance. This was the only time this has ever happened in my 20 years of teaching this material!

What I said apparently had offended the pastor of the church that was hosting our conference, because he did not attend any of the remaining sessions of our training. I did not know that he was an admirer of this American pastor and was actually patterning his preaching and ministry style after him. Fortunately, none of the other pastors and leaders attending the training seemed offended by my comments, and many of them were in agreement with what I said.

I began to wonder why I made those comments. Why did I say what I said when I never had before? While talking to my Nigerian host, who had arranged the training for us at this particular church, he told me that the church pastor was indeed following that path and needed to be rebuked for it. Obviously, the Holy Spirit was speaking to that pastor through me that day. He had a purpose and would use me to convey a message for Him, even a rebuking!

Over the years I have also had the opportunity to share about our training on radio and television. It was usually about our reason for being in the country we were in and what our training was all about. Some of them were Christian broadcasts and some were not. I have been interviewed on the radio in Albania, Ghana and Peru, and on television in Peru and Grenada. They are sometimes difficult to prepare for because they can come up unexpectedly, as one radio interview did in Peru.

But even when I have the chance to prepare, I don't always know all of the questions they might ask, and I really only get this one chance to articulate the gospel and the purpose of our ministry. I always pray before each of these opportunities and ask the Holy Spirit to give me the words to say, and to speak through me to accomplish His purpose for that interview. And I have always thought that He has done so.

Letting someone else speak for you is something you may find hard to do. You may be uncomfortable letting someone else speak on your behalf because they may not know your feelings or thoughts. Other times you don't speak at all because you don't know what to say. As a result, you just stay silent and say nothing. Others are then left to wonder what your opinion or thoughts are. Or perhaps you fear being misunderstood when you are not sure you will be able to say what you mean clearly enough. These are quite natural for all of us.

However, God is not just anybody. Letting God speak for you will not harm you because He wants His best for you. God knows what to say even when you don't. He will always speak the truth in love and will speak in ways that bring glory to Him. So, you should not be afraid to ask God to speak for you when you need Him to. Just pray for the Holy Spirit to speak for you and He will. God did this for Moses, He has done it for me, and He will do it for you as well!

Letting go of our words and letting the Holy Spirit speak for us is not always easy or comfortable. But I have always found His words to be better than mine, and they end up being a blessing for me as well.

Knowing that God and His Holy Spirit can speak through us is something that everyone can learn, and is a lesson we can all be blessed by!

Chapter 10

LESSON #8: GOD PROTECTS US

"You are my hiding place; you will protect me from trouble and surround me with songs of deliverance."
Psalm 32:7

Fear is a part of our everyday lives. We fear war, we fear cancer, we fear accidents, and we fear the unknown. The fact is – life is dangerous! There is danger all around us, although we try not to think about it. Some fear is healthy as it keeps us from harm or dangerous situations. But some fears can also be irrational and immobilize us. So, whether we like it or not, life is risky. There is always the possibility of danger. Some dangers we can see coming, but often they can hit us when we least expect it!

Jesus said that *"in this world you will have trouble."* (**John 16:33**) He was recognizing the fact that our world was filled with sin and sinful people that make it dangerous and unpredictable. He was saying that we <u>*will*</u> have troubles, not *might* have troubles. It is a fact of simply living on this earth! No one is exempt from trouble or danger.

As Christians we have other risks. Jesus told his disciples, *"If the world hates you, keep in mind it hated me first."* (**John 15:18**) He also goes on to tell them, *"If they persecuted me, they will persecute you also."* (**John 15:20**) He was warning His disciples about the risks they face in being associated with Him. The Apostle Paul told Timothy that *"In fact, everyone who wants to live a Godly life will be persecuted."* (**2 Timothy 3:12**) He too was acknowledging the truth that being a follower of Christ is risky and dangerous.

So, if living life is dangerous, and following Christ is risky, how are we as Christians supposed to respond to His call and purpose for our lives, especially when we fear the dangers and risks we might have to face?

I immediately think of Jonah and how God had called him to *"go to the great city of Nineveh and preach against it, because its wickedness has come up before me."* (**Jonah 1:2**) Jonah sensed the risk to his life and obviously did not want to go there out of fear of what might happen to him if he did. So how did Jonah respond to God's call? He ran away and ended up in the belly of a big fish for three days and three nights until he repented and obeyed.

Like Jonah, we too are sometimes afraid and want to run away and hide from doing what God wants us to do. So, how do we overcome our fear? We do that by remembering the following three truths about our life and the Lord.

First of all, <u>life holds no guarantees of safety</u>. Every human life faces danger and risk. We first faced it when we were born because there is a risk in childbirth. As we grew up, we faced the risks of illness, hunger, accidents or losing our parents. As adults we face risks from serious injuries, unemployment or financial problems.

And as we grow old, we face risks from loneliness, deteriorating health, and lack of activity. Currently the world is facing the risk of the COVID-19 virus pandemic. As a result, there is no guarantee we will be able to even breathe tomorrow.

We do not have control over our environment despite what some may think. The Bible puts it this way: *"Why, you do not even know what will happen tomorrow. What is your life? You are a mist that appears for a little while and then vanishes."* (**James 4:14**) It is not a very comforting thought, but it is the truth. Believing that we are safe in a world of danger and trouble is an illusion. We are never safe. There is always danger that we do not see and are not aware of. It can be random and just a matter of being in the wrong place at the wrong time. Let me share a story that illustrates what I mean.

A few months after we moved to Atlanta in 1998, there was an accident on GA 400, a major highway leading from downtown Atlanta to the north suburbs. It was not an accident between two cars as one might think. Instead, it was a plane crash on the highway. A small private plane had lost power before it reached the local airport and was descending over the crowded highway during the late afternoon rush hour. The lanes were completely full of cars and traffic was bumper to bumper.

Given the situation the pilot had no choice but to try his best to land on the highway between cars. According to the FAA report, the plane struck one car and pushed it off the highway before hitting a second car and coming to a stop. The pilot and the driver of the first car sustained relatively minor injuries, but the driver of the second car was killed.

It was a miracle that only one person died, and it wasn't even the pilot as one might expect. But for that one person who died, he was the wrong person in the wrong place at the wrong time. The driver may never have seen the plane coming if it was behind him, and it may not have mattered if he had. It was absolutely unforeseen and completely random. Out of the hundreds of cars on that highway at that specific place and time, it was one person, in one car, that was killed. I'm sure the driver never thought for a moment that something like this could happen to anyone, let alone him. These are the dangers in life that occur every day that we cannot predict. Life can be random, and it holds no guarantee of safety.

Second, <u>Jesus told us that he has overcome the world and its troubles</u>. Although Jesus said, *"In this world you will have trouble,"* he also said, *"But take heart! I have overcome the world."* (**John 16:33**) Through his death on the cross, Jesus paid for our sins and made it possible for us to have eternal life with Him and His Father in Heaven. Jesus overcame death and the grave so that we might experience the joy of eternal life and the freedom that comes with it. That freedom is the knowledge that we no longer need to fear death. Death is no longer the end of life, only the end of our physical life on this earth. Jesus took our death away from us so that we could live forever. This simple truth helps us to overcome our fears in this life.

Third, <u>God promises to protect us</u>. The Bible says, *"You are my hiding place; You will protect me from trouble."* (**Psalm 32:7**), and *"God is our refuge and strength, an ever-present help in trouble."* (**Psalm 46:1**) This is God's promise and assurance to us as believers and followers of His Son Jesus. God protected

Noah and his family from the flood. He protected David from Saul and his pursuers. He protected the Christian believers in Damascus from Saul's persecution. And He protects us today from the many troubles, dangers and risks we face, including the ones we never see.

I believe and know that God is my only protection in this world. I once returned from a trip to the Philippines and one of our church members said to me, *"Aren't you afraid of going to the Philippines? They just cut off the head of a missionary there. Isn't that too dangerous for you to take such a risk?"* Well, it was true that a missionary couple had been kidnapped by terrorists in the Philippines. When they tried to escape, the husband was caught and had his head cut off as punishment. Fortunately, his wife was able to escape. But that church member did not know the whole story.

This particular missionary couple were serving in a large and safe area of the Philippines and had received a gift a of a resort vacation on one of the outer islands. That island was known for its beaches and vacation amenities but also for the presence of terrorists. The missionaries probably should have known this and the danger they were putting themselves into by going to such a remote, isolated island where there were terrorists present.

The terrorists kidnapped them because they were Americans and thought to have money and wealth. But they were actually poor missionaries serving the Filipino people. The captors demanded a ransom, but the US government was not willing to pay them. Knowing their precarious situation, when the couple saw an opportunity to escape, they did. Unfortunately, only one of them made it to safety.

I told this church member that when I go to the Philippines, I go to a safe area that is far away from where this incident took place. I also said that Americans are appreciated in the Philippines and rarely attacked in general. I felt completely safe where I was and who I was with. It's like worrying about going to Florida when there are wildfires in California. Problems in one place do not necessarily translate into problems in another place, even if they are in the same country. As a matter of fact, I told them it was probably more dangerous for me to go into some of our own major cities in America than where I was ministering in the Philippines.

Unfortunately, the media in America tends to only report international news if the story is sensational (like this missionary couple), without really fully explaining the background or circumstances. As a result, Americans can get a false picture or impression of the nation or city in the news story.

This is true of many of the places I have traveled to over the years. I have been to some rugged places that many people think might be dangerous, including Egypt, Ukraine, Vietnam, Myanmar, Indonesia, Haiti, Nigeria and the Democratic Republic of Congo. But in each of them, I have generally felt safe once I spent a little time there and got to know the people and the culture. Our fears are often based on a lack of knowledge or misinformation.

But there are risks associated with being in any foreign country. These include things like getting sick, injuries, travel problems, accidents, earthquakes, local strikes, and political instability. I never know what emergencies might come up. However, these are all things that can happen in my country as well. But if I dwell on these things too much, I would never go any-where, and that's not rational either.

I always assess the risk of where I am going and read the State Department travel warnings and advisories to educate myself. I have also established a policy of not going to nations that have a high warning level based on State Department guidelines. In other words, I am not going to go to a nation where I might put myself at considerable risk (North Korea or Syria, for example). Fortunately, only a small number of nations carry this designation.

I will also admit that I've had my share of dangerous situations in the nations I have been to. For the most part, these situations were just the regular dangers of life in this world. The things I experienced could easily have happened to me in the USA. But the fact that they happened in a foreign country where I did not speak the language or know the correct cultural response made them a bit more challenging. Without that kind of knowledge, I had to rely on our host (if they were with me at the time) and the Holy Spirit. There was no other option.

But these situations all taught me one thing – God is my protector! He alone has protected me from every danger I've faced! Here are some stories from a few of those situations where I felt God's Spirit of protection.

On our first trip to the Philippines in 1997 we held one of our training conferences up in the mountains in a tiny village called Mayoyao. We were on a bus owned by the ministry and there were about 25 of us, both Americans and Filipinos, making the trip from Tabuk up to the village. As night fell, we were headed up the mountain and it started to rain. We were on a dirt road that wound its way up the mountain. Our bus driver would accelerate when he got to the straight part of the road and when we reached the curve he would apply the brakes and the bus would slide around the curve due to the muddy condition of the road. There was no guardrail and I could just envision the newspaper headlines: *"AMERICAN MISSIONARY TEAM KILLED AS BUS SLIDES OFF A MOUNTAIN IN THE PHILIPPINES!"*

After several of these turns many of the American passengers began to feel some anxiety about the safety of the bus and our team (apparently this speed was normal for Filipinos but quite unsettling for us). They expressed this to our team leader who then approached the bus driver and asked him to please slow down. Fortunately, the driver complied, but he was still driving too fast for me. So, I just closed my eyes because I didn't want to look how close to going off the road we were. We made it safely to our destination that night thanks to God's protection of our team!

We also ran into danger on the way down the mountain when we encountered a portion of the road that had slid down the mountainside in the previous days of rain. There was literally just enough of the road left for the bus to pass (by inches!). We debated for a while whether to turn back, but given the time of the day it was best that we go on. We could not get off the bus either, because there was no room on the road for us to step onto, just a five hundred yard drop into a canyon below!

So, we all moved to the left side of the bus as the driver slowly and carefully drove over what was left of the road. On our left was the side of the mountain and on the right was the deep drop into the canyon. It was a very tight squeeze, but we made it through and were very much relieved. God was watching over us and protecting us once again!

As we came off the mountain, we stopped for dinner in a town at the base of the mountains before heading back on the normal highway to Tabuk, where we had come from a few days earlier. It was late and very dark driving back. As a result of the tension of the day and a good dinner, most everyone fell asleep on the bus.

We had been driving for a while when all of a sudden the bus hit something. It jerked up and down and people went flying up in the air. Some hit the ceiling and others hit the windows, the other seats, or other people around them. Fortunately for me, I was holding on to a bar that kept me from hitting the ceiling. The bus driver stopped to see if everyone was okay. One of the Filipinos hurt their wrist, but by God's grace everyone else was uninjured.

What we learned that night is that on some roads in the Philippines the concrete sections of the roadway sometimes do not meet, and that leaves a three to six inch gap in the roadway. It results from a lack of roadway funding, city or province boundary lines, or simply poor planning. Our driver did not see the gap in time and hit it going about 50 miles per hour. It was pretty scary and unexpected. But once again, God protected us from potential major injuries.

Some of the other dangers I've faced include accidents, which are common in any country. On one trip to the Philippines, we were leaving our host's home after breakfast to go to the church to begin our training. His adult son was driving us in his minivan. One of my team members was in the front passenger seat and I and another team member were in the back seat. It was raining lightly that morning and the roads were wet. They also lived at a curve in the road.

As he pulled the van up to the road to turn onto it, there was a cement truck to the right of us that was just coming around the curve. As we waited for the truck to pass by it suddenly lost control on the wet pavement, began to slide, and came right at us. We had no time to move or get out of the way. It hit us with a glancing blow near the front passenger side of the van. The driver and I were alright, but my two friends on that side of the van were pretty shaken up. They were bruised and had minor cuts from flying glass. Fortunately, there were no serious injuries. But it could have been much worse. God had protected us all!

Another accident I was in happened on a trip to India in 2013. My training partner and I were on the way to the airport in the town of Raipur for our flight that day to Hyderabad. We were in a car owned by the hotel where we had stayed the night before. They were providing our transportation to the airport.

We were approaching a large intersection and the traffic light was green, so our driver proceeded through the intersection. But then the light turned yellow and all of a sudden something hit the right side of our car. It was a man on a motorcycle who had "jumped" the light and slammed right into the driver side of our car. Our driver immediately pulled over and got out to check on the motorcyclist, who was lying on the road.

The next thing we knew there was a crowd of very angry people gathered around our car yelling at the driver and looking very menacing. They were speaking in Hindi, but we could tell they were blaming our driver for the accident and seemed to want to inflict their own justice. We did not know what to do except to stay in the car and pray.

Fortunately, there was a police officer directing traffic at the intersection who saw everything. He came over to our car and calmed the crowd down. We then saw an ambulance come and take the motorcyclist away. This all happened within five minutes of the accident (it turns out there was a hospital right near the intersection). Our driver told the officer that he was taking us to the airport. Since we were Americans, the officer allowed him to do that on the condition that he came right back and made a statement. So, we were very blessed to escape injury and be able to make our flight as well. God was indeed our protector!

Another dangerous situation that required God's protection happened on a trip I had mentioned earlier when I led a team from a church in Knoxville, TN to the town of Trujillo, Peru in 2007. We had been ministering to the community for several days doing evangelism, construction and children's ministry. On one evening our team was invited to attend a worship service at a Messianic church in one of the barrios, a poor area of the city. The worship service was held right out in the street on a stage that was set up for it. We sang some Spanish worship songs for them and one of our team members preached the message that night.

During the sermon, one of our translators, a young man of about nineteen years, came over to me as the team leader and said we have to leave right away. He said there was a shooting in the neighborhood and it wasn't safe for us to stay there. He was definitely scared. We had already been invited to stay after the service to have some fellowship time with the local church leaders, and so I was reluctant to leave abruptly at that moment, especially since the sermon wasn't over yet. But I did promise him that after the sermon we would leave as quickly as possible.

I then turned around to look at the people there, and no one seemed worried or anxious to leave. I don't think anyone heard a gunshot, and if they did, they apparently did not feel it necessary to get out of the street. There were children all around us playing in the street and so I thought that this could not be as dangerous as our young translator thought. But we needed to be cautious because we were visitors and foreigners.

We had a very brief time of fellowship with tea and cookies after the service was over. We told our hosts that because of the shooting we needed to leave right away.

We said our goodbyes and we all got on our bus to leave. Our translator then came on the bus and said that the police were coming, and they told us to wait there and they would escort us out of the area.

As the team leader, I was concerned that some of our team members might be afraid or stressed about our circumstances. I looked around our bus and everyone was smiling and laughing and did not seem worried or troubled at all. Outside the bus there were dozens of people thanking us and smiling at us, even many children. Once again, I thought this can't be as dangerous as one might think if the local people aren't worried or concerned.

Eventually the police arrived and escorted us out of the neighborhood. But during the entire time we felt safe and not threatened at all. God was certainly protecting our team from danger and also calming us during the situation. As the team leader, I was very grateful for the Holy Spirit's presence and protection!

One of the more common risky situations I have faced on mission trips is meeting our hosts for the first time when I arrive in their country. I have been doing this for many years, but this happened mostly in the early years of our ministry. I would arrive at an airport and expect to be picked up by my host, who was usually someone I met through email. I did not even know what they looked like. I also did not have a cell phone back then nor did our host. They would usually hold up a sign with my name on it, and I would go to them when I came out of the terminal with my baggage. I don't do that as often anymore because of the widespread use of the internet and cell phones today. But it amazes me that I did that when I think back on it! I was very trusting in the Lord and He protected me every time!

Regardless of the circumstances I have faced when traveling in other nations, I always knew that God was there and would protect me from danger and harm. And He has never failed to do so. Sure, I'm a little older and wiser now than when I first started, but it's always comforting to know that God and His Spirit are by my side no matter what I face. As the Scripture says, *"The Lord is my light and my salvation – whom shall I fear? The Lord is the stronghold of my life – of whom shall I be afraid?"* (**Psalm 27:1**)

God is ready and able to protect you as well from the dangers and risks that you face in your life. While you may not travel to other countries or work and live in a dangerous environment, you will nevertheless encounter dangers and risks, many of which you may never see. But putting your trust in God enables you to live in faith and not in fear. Knowing God is protecting you allows you to live freely and abundantly. But you should also communicate with God through the Holy

Spirit so that you heed his voice and avoid the dangers that could potentially harm you. Listening to God and trusting in Him will give you His peace and protection in any situation.

When God is on our side, we have the courage to face dangers, risks, and even our fear. God will protect us by His Holy Spirit, and He always has our back!

Chapter 11

LESSON #9: GOD CARRIES US

*"Cast all your anxiety on Him
because He cares for you."*
1 Peter 5:7

Growing up in America, there were two things I was taught from an early age. One, I could be whatever I wanted to be in life. There were no limitations on what I could achieve, if I worked hard enough and put my mind to it. Anyone could become President of the United States one day if they so desired. Two, I was to be responsible for myself. That meant I was to pull my own weight in life and not be a burden to others. I was taught to work hard, rely on my own abilities, and to not become dependent on anyone else. These were typical values for most Americans, especially males, and were derived from our historical foundation of liberty and freedom to pursue our own interests, along with a strong Puritan work ethic.

These values were reinforced at home, and in public school, and provided the foundation for the lives and careers we would eventually pursue. Because I grew up in a middle-income suburb of Chicago, most of my high school classmates went on to college and earned degrees. Some of them became doctors and lawyers, others achieved successful business careers, a few pursued athletic careers, and the rest enjoyed jobs as teachers, nurses, public servants and a variety of other professions. We all seemed to prosper as a result of the foundation of these two values that were built into our lives.

But the reality for me, and most of my classmates, was that education and hard work only got us so far, and that it often takes more than that to achieve the lofty goals in life we had set. As far as I know, none of my classmates has achieved the national success or noto-riety that some of them had sought. I have yet to see any of their names on the national news or occupying important positions in business, government, academia, sports, entertainment or the media. That doesn't mean that their lives were not successful, just that they may not have achieved the original goals they aspired to.

I enjoyed a long business career but never achieved the goals I set for myself and had pursued. I eventually ended up starting and managing a global training min-istry that brought me immense joy and satisfaction, but not much notoriety.

But that's okay. I never really had lofty goals to become President of the United States, CEO of a major business, or become famous one day. I had simple goals to have a successful business career and a family. And God provided both of those to me, for which I am very thankful.

But even those things that I had achieved were not the result of my hard work alone. They often resulted from God's hand on my life, as I detailed in my first book about my journey of faith. And while it is easy to claim that I did it all by myself, that would not be the truth. In reality, there were many times God carried me through situations and helped me overcome obstacles.

I remember seeing a poster once entitled "Footprints." You probably have heard of it or have seen it. It shows two sets of footprints walking along a beach and then one set of footprints disappears. The text on the poster asks why Jesus stopped walking with them at a particularly difficult time in their life. Jesus' response was that His footprints were not the ones that disappeared, but it was when He was carrying us through our difficult times. That image and text have stuck with me all these years. It reminds me that God will *"never leave us or forsake us"* (**Hebrews 13:5**) and that Jesus promises that He will *"always be with us to the very end of the age."* (**Matthew 28:20**).

I have experienced the Lord carrying me several times on mission trips over the years. They usually occurred when I was in unfamiliar situations or circumstances beyond my control. And the fact that they occurred in a foreign country only added to my inability to come up with a solution on my own. Most of the time, there was no solution except to bear the burden until it resolved itself.

Perhaps the most common had to do with our lodging. While I never had to sleep in a tent, most of my accommodations were simple and comfortable. But there were several that were quite challenging.

On a few of our early trips to the Philippines we slept in an upstairs bedroom with no air conditioning, fan or window. It was brutally hot which made it difficult to sleep. There was also no hot water for our showers and on one trip the shower only had ice cold mountain water. Brrr!

On the other extreme there were trips to Peru where we experienced hotel rooms with no heat and no hot water in temperatures that fell to freezing or below at night! On one trip to Peru and one trip to the Democratic Republic of Congo we had no running water at all!

But through these experiences I learned one thing. After a day or two of that our bodies and minds adjust to the new norm. It no longer became the burden it was on the first day. God created our bodies to be somewhat adaptable to our surroundings. God indeed had carried us through these times!

Another common situation that we face in other countries is the lack of what we Americans consider good bathroom facilities. When we stayed in hotels or guest houses, we normally had clean and comfortable bathrooms. But when we were gone during the day to train or minister in communities, that was rarely the case.

One of my earliest experiences with a really bad bathroom was in Bishkek, Kyrgyzstan in 1999. We were holding a worship conference in a large public auditorium in the center of the city. I remember asking one of my mission team members one day where the bathroom was. They told me to *"go to the main lobby and take the central stairway that goes down. Then just follow the smell!"* How right they were! It was perhaps the most unsanitary and awful bathroom I have ever been in, anywhere. And for a male, that's saying something! Needless to say, I tried to avoid the bathroom there the rest of my time in Bishkek!

I've also experienced either the lack of a bathroom altogether or just having a hole in the ground to use. This was more typical in Africa and Asia if we were in remote areas or small villages. Because I wear a colostomy bag, it can become a real challenge for me at times, because I can't always predict when I will need to use a bathroom to empty the bag. As a result, I began to pray each morning before I would leave the hotel. I would ask the Holy Spirit to let me make it through the day without having to empty my bag until I got back to our hotel that night. And God answered that prayer almost every time! The same is true for those long flights overseas. God always carried me through those situations, and I was always thankful to Him for that!

Another type of experience that often occurs on mission trips is illness. For me, that usually meant a head cold. But there were several times when I had stomach problems, flu symptoms or other ailments. Most of my colds seemed to occur on my way back home. I think it's because when I arrive in a foreign country my adrenaline is keeping me going due to the excitement or apprehension of what it is going to be like. But once I settle in and get adjusted to the time zone, food and lodging, the adrenaline starts to wear off. Many mission trips are also exhausting, and so I don't always sleep well either.

Consequently, towards the end of the trip my immune system weakens, and I pick up a cold. Many times, when I arrive at the airport for the flight home, I start to get the chills, sore throat, and body aches. On a few of these occasions I was miserable. But at least it was easier to tolerate knowing I would be home soon where I can rest and recover.

In my opinion, there is nothing worse than to have stomach problems while traveling away from home. And it doesn't matter whether a person is in their own nation or another one. It is just plain awful. I have had stomach problems on several occasions while in another nation on a mission trip. Most of the time it was due to the food I had eaten that was probably washed in the local water, which would normally result in stomach cramps for 24 hours. Some of them were severe enough to keep me from training on a few trips. Although I tried to be very careful about what I ate, sometimes it is hard to tell what food might be tainted.

I also came down with the flu once in Peru while staying with American missionaries in their home. Fortunately, my training partner had brought some cold and flu medicine that really helped, and I was able to be back on my feet in a couple of days. It also did not impact my training either. Since then I learned to take several over the counter cold and flu medicines with me on every trip so that I would be prepared! But each time I was ill, God either saw me through it or provided a person to train in my place. Again, God carried me through my illnesses!

Perhaps the most painful experience I have ever had was a pulled muscle in my back. The first time I experienced this was as a senior in high school. It happened while I was wearing some weighted vests while playing basketball to build up my upper body strength. It took several weeks to heal and required stretching exercises and rest. It almost jeopardized my senior basketball season. I just remember how painful it was to walk, sit, sleep or get comfortable.

It happened again in 2010 as I was getting ready to leave on a mission trip to Rwanda and the Democratic Republic of Congo. Two days before the trip, I was moving some boxes in my office and pulled a muscle in my back. I went down in a heap on the floor. I could barely move, let alone get up off the floor or walk. It felt just like the time I pulled a back muscle in high school and I knew the recovery would take time. But the trip had been scheduled for months and paid for too. My hosts had made all of the necessary preparations and my training partner was eager to go as well. So, I got a cane and decided to make the trip and rely on God to see me through it.

While the flight and riding in a car were painful, I managed to get by. But every time I got out of my air-line seat or the car seat, I had to use the cane just to stand up and take the first few steps. The more I walked, though, the muscle would relax and I could walk okay. My back also got a little better each day the more I moved around and stretched that muscle. But it was difficult and sometimes quite painful.

It happened to me again in 2017 a few days before a trip to the Ukraine. I was playing with my granddaughter, who was making chalk drawings on a driveway. I bent down to draw with her for at least twenty minutes, and when I stood up, my back began to bother me. By the time I had driven home that night I was in serious back pain again. Having been on a mission trip with a back problem before I knew I could survive, so I went ahead and made the trip. I took my cane again and prayed that it would not get any worse. Like the trip in 2010, God certainly carried me!

Despite lodging issues, bad bathrooms and travel challenges, God's Spirit goes with us to carry us when needed. Even when my stomach, my body or my back failed me, God did not. And I learned to rely on Him when I did not have the strength to rely on myself. God truly carries us, even when we may not realize it!

How has God carried you in your life? I would imagine that you could look back and reflect on the difficult times in your life when God has carried you. Did you know it at the time, or did you realize it later? Did you ask Him to carry you or did He just do that on His own?

When you stop and think about it, it really doesn't matter. The important point to remember is that He loves you and cares for you so deeply that He is willing to take your burdens upon Himself and carry them for your sake. And He does that willingly and without hesitation! So why not let Him? You will be amazed at how He lifts your burdens and gives you comfort!

Chapter 12

LESSON #10: GOD IS ALWAYS FAITHFUL

"For the word of the Lord is right and true;
He is faithful in all He does."
Psalm 33:4

When we enter our world as a baby, we have no alternative but to trust others. Initially we put our trust in the doctors and nurses who delivered us. Then we begin to put our trust in our parents, and maybe other family members, like siblings and grandparents. Next, we start to grow and learn about trusting our friends or playmates. And when we begin school, we must learn to trust our teachers, school officials, coaches and others in authority. So, as we grow up, we are constantly learning who in our lives is trustworthy, so we know who to trust as we get older.

As an infant, we do not really decide about whom to trust. We have to trust whoever cares and provides for us because we have no other alternative. But as we grow, we start learning about trust and who we can put our trust in. Sadly, some children learn that they can't trust their parents, which can result in lifelong struggles with trust issues. Others learn that they cannot trust people in authority or those they do not know. Some of us have had a trust broken so we don't trust anyone. The point is, as we grow, we are learning about trust and who is trustworthy in our own eyes. For many of us, the only person we really trust is ourselves!

As a result, who or what we put our trust in becomes the foundation of our lives. It often starts with *who* we trust. If we only put our trust in ourselves then we will live a self-focused and self-dependent life that relies on no one else, because no one else is trustworthy in our eyes. If we put our trust in somebody else, like scientists, then we live and die by what scientists tell us, because no one other than scientists are trustworthy.

For most people, though, we selectively choose who to put our trust in. It depends on our experience with people, be they parents, teachers, scientists, or others. If we believe that what other people tell us is true, or we experience it ourselves, then we tend to trust them.

In addition, we also decide *what* to put our trust in. It may be our education, our skills, or our life experiences. It all depends upon what has proven to be trustworthy in the past. But what if we learn that what we were taught in school was not completely true? What if we discover that what we thought was accurate really wasn't? How do we know if what we know, or have experienced, is actually true and worthy of our trust?

Back in the 1990's there was a movie called *The Matrix*. The premise of the movie is that there is an alternate world to our own that we don't see called the Matrix. It starred Keanu Reeves as Neo and Lawrence Fishburne as Morpheus. Neo is a computer hacker who discovers that there is a force controlling the earth, and that he was not truly free. He encounters Morpheus, a rebel, who offers him the opportunity to experience this other world and to join their effort to give humans back control of their own reality. He offers Neo a choice. He can take a blue pill and go on living as he had been. Or he can take a red pill and be shown the truth of the Matrix. Neo chose the red pill.

We have a similar, yet different, choice today. There is life on this earth that we all experience because we are physically here. But there is another world that we can experience that exists in parallel with ours. What world is that? It's the spiritual world. And that world is governed by God, who created our earthly world. The difference between the Matrix and our world is that God has given us free will to choose which reality we want to experience. We can put our trust in man, or ourselves, and what we can see or experience in this physical world (blue pill), or we can put our trust in God and see and experience the spiritual world (red pill). I have chosen to know God! Which would you choose?

The great thing about putting our trust in God instead of our world is that we get to experience both at the same time. If we put our trust in the physical world we will only experience its pleasures and its sinfulness. We will never get to experience the joy and blessings that only His Spirit can provide.

But if we put our trust and faith in God, we can experience His truth and love in the spiritual realm while also enjoying His creation and blessings while we live on this earth! We get the best of both worlds! If we only trust in our earthly world, then we will ultimately be let down by both it, and people, because they are both sinful and not trustworthy. Only God is faithful and true.

God's Word tells us that *"all have sinned and fall short of the glory of God."* (**Romans 3:23**) People are sinners and therefore cannot be fully trusted. We all are born with a sinful nature that tends to cause us to focus on what is good for us and not others. That sometimes causes us to lie, which in turn makes us untrustworthy. The Bible also says, *"For everything in the world – the cravings of sinful man, the lust of his eyes and the boasting of what he has and does–does not come from the Father but from the world."* (**1 John 2:16**) We also live in a corrupt world that seeks to corrupt us. How can we put our trust in a world so filled with deceit and corruption? Our world is far from trustworthy as well.

The only one worthy of our trust is God. The Bible says that God is faithful. *"The word of the Lord is right and true; He is faithful in all He does."* (**Psalm 33:4**) The Bible also says that He speaks the truth. *"I, the Lord, speak the truth; I declare what is right."* (**Isaiah 45:19**). He is the only one we can fully trust, because He alone is trustworthy!

The Bible also says He is faithful to keep His promises to us. *"The Lord is faithful to all His promises and loving toward all He has made."* (**Psalm 145:13**) If we put our trust in ourselves or in others, we will eventually be let down because people are flawed and sinful. But if we put our trust in God, we will never be let down and never left to figure things out on our own. He will guide and direct us and give us His wisdom to overcome any obstacles we face in our life.

Learning that God is always faithful is an important spiritual lesson for any follower of Christ. But it is also important for every human to know as well. For when we know and trust God, we have someone who will always be there for us. We have someone who will help us persevere through any trial we face. And we have someone who will *"never leave us or forsake us"* (**Hebrews 13:5**) either.

Sharing specific experiences from my mission travels about God's faithfulness is somewhat difficult because He is always faithful! In other words, some problems never arose because God had already taken care of them before they happened. And for the problems that did occur, He helped us to overcome them. So, in reality, the absence of problems or difficulties, and the overcoming of them, is in itself a testimony to God's faithfulness in having everything proceed according to His will. But I can share some of the ways that I know that God has been faithful to our ministry over the years.

As mentioned at the beginning of this book, in my 24 years of mission travel I have been on 137 trips to 50 nations. Throughout those years there were less than a handful of trips that I had to cancel because of the lack of funds, health issues or other problems. But I also believe that God's Spirit prevented me from going to protect me in some way. Although I may never know why, I do know that God prevented Paul from going to Asia to preach the Word. The Bible tells us, *"Paul and his companions traveled throughout the region of Phrygia and Galatia, having been kept by the Holy Spirit from preaching the Word in the province of Asia."* (**Acts 16:6**) God has His reasons, and that is good enough for me!

God has also been faithful in keeping me from sickness, except for a few trips. When one considers the many time zones, cultures and foods I have experienced, it's amazing that I have been healthy during the vast majority of the trips I have taken. I've even taken trips where I was not at full strength. Yet God gave me the strength to endure them and complete the training He had planned for me.

In 2007 I was having some intestinal problems before a trip to Kenya but felt that I was well enough to go. But three days after I returned home I found myself in the emergency room at our local hospital with severe abdominal pain. It turned out to be a blocked colon which eventually required surgery and 21 days in the hospital. It also resulted in my having to wear a colostomy bag which I mentioned earlier. If that had happened in Kenya I cannot imagine what I would have experienced there, especially without my family, my doctor, and church around to give me peace and comfort. I was grateful that God was faithful and brought me home first!

God has also protected me from harm on all of our mission trips. I have not sustained any injuries on any of the trips I have taken that I can recall. I had no bruises, no broken bones, and no scrapes. Not even a jammed finger or twisted ankle! It's pretty amazing when you consider the many places and facilities I've been in where the opportunity for an injury was present. I've walked up and down steep mountains, been bounced around in a bus on the roadway, had a few near accidents, and had several slips and falls. And through it all, God has kept me safe and injury free so that I could do the work He had called me to.

We often take things like these for granted because it's what we expect. But the truth is that God watches over us like a hen watches over her chicks so that we can accomplish what He sent us to do.

One of the ways God has also proven faithful is by the generally smooth logistics of what had been needed to hold our training conferences in other countries.

Whether it was training manual copying, food preparation, organizing facilities for the training, providing interpreters, arranging lodging or transportation, it has mostly gone on without any major problems. This is not always easy considering language barriers, local circumstances, currency differences, and cultural nuances that make communication difficult sometimes. But through all the trips I've made for training, we have always been able to overcome problems and mistakes so that the training could be effective. And we owe that to God, who oversees our plans and needs and provides what is needed when we need it.

God has also proved faithful in providing finances for our ministry for 20 years. When we needed to raise a salary to cover our living expenses to work full-time in this ministry, God provided a bank and its president to support us. A few years later, the bank folded and then God sent us new supporters to replace them. When we needed additional funds to support our global trainer network, God once again directed others to meet those needs. While we have had to trim our budget every so often, God has never failed to provide for us and this ministry. Knowing that God is faithful allows us to put our trust in Him, have peace in our circumstances, and know that He will supply what is needed according to His purpose and plan.

Another way that God has been faithful to our ministry is by giving us wisdom and discernment in our decision making. Because this is God's ministry, we try to seek His wisdom for what to pursue and how to pursue it. God has given us direction and guidance when we have requested it. As a result, our trips have been fruitful and blessed. I am sure that if we had gone against His counsel, we would have experienced problems and difficulties of our own making. Because our trips have gone so well, I can only attribute that to God's presence and blessing in following His guidance and direction.

God has proven faithful to us and our ministry. He has always provided, protected, and guided us on the path He wanted us to take. By placing our faith and trust in Him, we have prospered as a ministry. By allowing the Holy Spirit to work through us, great things have been accomplished in His name, and we have been blessed immeasurably in the process. We are grateful to God for His love for us and His faith in us to carry out the work He has entrusted to us.

I would encourage you to make a list of the many ways God has been faithful to you in your life. Thinking about those times and writing them down will enable you to see that God has been involved in your life more than you may have previously realized. He will likely reveal other times He was faithful to you as well which will help you to understand the depth of His love for you. It is my hope and prayer that this simple exercise will lead you to a stronger faith and a greater trust in His promises.

God is always faithful to those who call upon Him!

EPILOGUE

*"Now the Lord is Spirit, and where the Spirit of the
Lord is, there is freedom. And we, who with unveiled
faces all reflect the Lord's glory, are being trans
formed into His likeness with ever increasing glory,
which comes from the Lord, who is Spirit."*
2 Corinthians 3:17-18

Through my numerous international mission field experiences, I have witnessed God's Spirit at work in my life and ministry. God has taught me that He alone is sufficient for my needs, and that His Spirit is always available when I call upon Him. Through His Holy Spirit, God works to bring about His purposes, His will, and His plans through me. He also does the same for all who would call upon His name.

It is my hope that through the stories and testimonies that I have shared in this book, you will begin to see how God intersects in your life every single day. When you call upon His Holy Spirit, you will develop spiritual eyes that enable you to see what you have not seen before. God is not absent or far away. He is right beside you waiting for you to turn to Him for whatever you may need. He hears your prayers, He provides for you, He protects you, and He carries you. And He does this because He loves you more than you may realize.

These 10 spiritual lessons that I have shared are not only for followers of Christ, but for all people. They are based on God's truth and were meant for all of His creation. These spiritual truths show us God's power, His character, and His love for everyone he created. He longs for everyone to turn to Him and allow His Spirit to guide and direct their lives. But so often we choose to go our own way and rely on our own abilities. Ultimately, the choice is ours whether to trust God and put our faith in Jesus, or to trust in man or ourselves to navigate this life. So, it comes down to a matter of faith and what we believe.

For non-Christians, they need the Holy Spirit to see and accept that God exists, that His Word is Truth, and that they can put their faith and trust in Him instead of themselves or this world. Like Neo in the Matrix, they must see that there is another reality beyond this earth. The Bible says that to do so they only need to look around and consider what they see. It says, *"For since the creation of the world God's invisible qualities – his eternal power and divine nature – have been clearly seen, being understood from what has been made, so that men are without excuse."* (**Romans 1:20**) They can only see this, however, with spiritual eyes. They must allow the Holy Spirit to enter their hearts so that they can be transformed by Him and see the spiritual reality that followers of Christ see and know.

For those of us who follow Christ, we cannot just say we have faith in Jesus. We must also live for Jesus and allow God's Spirit to help us to do that. That means that as followers we must obey his commands, let his Holy Spirit guide us, and seek to grow in our likeness of Him. The Bible says, *"Do not merely listen to the Word, and so deceive yourselves. Do what it says."* (**James**

1:22) It's not enough to just believe in Jesus. His followers must become more like Jesus!

To do that, they must also learn to live by the Holy Spirit as Jesus did. It was the Holy Spirit that gave Him his power to heal, to teach, to love and to die for us. Without the Holy Spirit, we are powerless to do anything. Jesus declares, *"Apart from me you can do nothing."* (**John 15:5**) If we want to live Spirit-filled lives and experience the abundant life that Jesus offers, we must submit our lives to the Holy Spirit and let Him lead and guide us through this life.

Unlike Neo in the Matrix, we don't have to choose a pill to swallow. Instead, God has given each of us the free will to make our own choice. We can choose to seek Him and follow Jesus, or we can choose to reject Him, and follow our own desires.

But the Bible is clear on the consequences of that choice. Jesus said, *"God so loved the world that He gave His one and only Son, that whoever believes in Him shall not perish but have eternal life."* (**John 3:16**) Choosing to follow Jesus produces a life that does not end in death, but instead promises us a life spent eternally with God.

Conversely, the Bible says, *"There is a way that seems right to a man, but in the end it leads to death."* (**Proverbs 14:12**) Choosing to follow our own ways, or those of the world, leads to a life that ends in death and a separation from God for all eternity.

Those who reject God are spiritually blind. They do not see God nor can they honor Him. Those who reject Jesus also reject God. Jesus also said, *"If you really knew me, you would know my Father as well."* (**John 14:7**)

The Scriptures tell us that the only way we can submit to God is through His Holy Spirit. We can't submit to God through our own power. As a matter of fact, we can't even believe in Jesus without the Holy Spirit. Jesus said, *"No one can come to me unless the Father who sent me draws him, and I will raise him up at the last day."* (**John 6:44**) God the Father draws us to Jesus through His Holy Spirit.

Finally, I hope that these 10 spiritual lessons that I have learned reveal to you how God's Spirit is at work in all of our lives. If you are a follower of Christ, I hope that they encourage you to seek Him more fervently and purposefully. I also pray that they would lead you to not only recognize the work of the Holy Spirit in your life, but give you a greater desire for Him as well.

If you are not a follower of Jesus, I hope that they inspire you to seek God, draw closer to Him through Jesus, and submit your life to the Holy Spirit. I pray that you don't follow the path of Satan and his lies and choose to put your trust in man, science, or the things of this world.

Instead, I pray that you would seek the Lord and let your eyes see the reality that so many people cannot see – that there is a God who not only loves you, but chooses you and is reaching out to you. He desires to have you know Him and live with Him for eternity through what His Son Jesus did in our world to save us from ourselves.

I further encourage you to let the Holy Spirit lead you to Jesus so that you can *"taste and see that the Lord is good!"* (**Psalm 34:8**) Then you can experience the abundant life that God intended for every human being. You will also receive the assurance that death is not the end, but the beginning of a wonderful, abundant, pain-free life in Heaven with God, Jesus and all the saints that have gone before us.

There is only one thing stopping you from that experience. It is your own choice to reject it. I pray that you will open your heart and mind so that you can receive God's Spirit! Because when you receive the Holy Spirit, you can know the Lord and experience the kind of life He intended for you all along!

ACKNOWLEDGEMENTS

There have been many people and experiences that have impacted my life and faith in Jesus. The mission field experiences that I have shared in this book do not mention all of the people I have met there that impacted my faith. Most of them perhaps don't even know it! But I believe that the Holy Spirit was working through all of them to help me see God more clearly and follow Jesus more completely. They were all *"links in the chain"* of my faith that encouraged me in my journey. Each one had a small part to play.

So, I thank God for all of the people that I met in the mission field, traveled with me to the mission field, or encouraged me in this mission ministry. They allowed the Holy Spirit to work through them to teach me these lessons.

I would specifically like to thank my wife, Kim, for her encouragement and spiritual wisdom that helped me in writing this book. I would also like to thank Ken, Erwin and Bob, who took the time to review the manuscript and provide helpful insights and suggestions that I know improved the content.

But most of all I continue to thank Jesus. He saved my life and called me according to His purpose.

To God alone be the glory!